The Neurotic Woman's Guide to Nonfulfillment

The Neurotic Woman's Guide to Nonfulfillment

Joy Kennedy

A Richard Seaver Book
The Viking Press / New York

A Richard Seaver Book / The Viking Press
First published in 1976 by The Viking Press, Inc.
625 Madison Avenue, New York, N.Y. 10022
Published simultaneously in Canada by
The Macmillan Company of Canada Limited
Printed in U.S.A.

Library of Congress Cataloging in Publication Data
Kennedy, Joy.
    The neurotic woman's guide to nonfulfillment.
    "A Richard Seaver book."
    1. Women—Psychology.   2. Interpersonal relations.
3. Women—Sexual behavior.   I. Title.
HQ1206.K42   155.6′33   73-17679
ISBN 0-670-50619-2

to Jackie Zimmermann

With special thanks to the magnificent seven without whom this book would have been neurotically postponed or languishing unfinished in my urgent agenda heap:

Alex Banks, research volunteer and other half
The other Kennedy sisters:
Fellow author, world shaker, attorney Flo Kennedy
Fellow author and invaluable critic Faye Kennedy Daly
Stabilizing influences Grayce Kennedy Bayles and Evelyn
    Kennedy Woods
and Dick and Jeanette Seaver, the world's most patient
    editors, conservatively speaking

Contents

Contents

Introduction

This book is based on the premise that most women who claim to be baffled at their lack of success with men actually have a subconscious, neurotic need to alienate and be rejected by them. Since their methods are largely unorganized and haphazard, however, women are frequently frustrated in their desire to experience what I have termed Complete Rejection Fulfillment, or CRF.

Therefore, in the belief that it should be the inalienable right of every woman to enjoy *maximum* fulfillment in this area, this book was written. Many of you may think that you are already experts at losing men, given your accumulated statistics in didn't-call-back prospects, died-on-the-vine romances, and love affairs that ended disastrously. You may feel that your present counterproductive methods and self-defeating attitudes provide you with adequate fulfillment of your rejection needs. But in most cases, while your history may show aptitude and promise, and you may feel satisfied, chances are you lack the knowledge, focus, and coordinated program that can be gleaned from this book. It was compiled on the basis of extensive in-depth interviews, eyeball statistics, word-of-mouth evidence, and similar scientific research conducted among successful failures of every ilk and description. By way of credentials, and not in any spirit of braggadocio, I submit that my own experiences, neurotically alienating men in three languages, nine countries, and five islands, make me uniquely qualified in the field.

This said, I must admit that, contrary to some opinion, I have not personally tested every recipe and method included herein (due more to the limits of time and physical capacity than lack of inclination). However, I feel confident that I can match my neurotic record of alienating men with that of any "How to" author, from J to Z.

At this point some of you may be asking: Why the need for rejection? Why should I or anyone else have a need to alienate men and be rejected by them? (Or some of the more liberation-minded among you may be asking: Why attribute the failure of relations to neuroses in women? What about the immature, inconstant, sexist, neurotic nature of men?)

Admittedly, as Freud concluded, no human being is without some form of neurosis. And since even the most confirmed male chauvinist would admit that women are human, it's obvious we come by our neuroses both naturally and inevitably. As for the specific neurotic need to be rejected by men, possible subconscious reasons are many and varied. But since any in-depth study of them would necessitate a book in itself, let us consider only some of the most common ones:

1. Feelings of guilt—for real or imagined transgressions—and a belief that happiness is undeserved (or that self-punishment is in order).

2. Feelings of insecurity and a to-know-me-would-be-not-to-love-me attitude, therefore a reject-before-rejected determination.

3. A subconscious fear of sex, pregnancy, or other such possible responsibilities.

4. A reluctance to sacrifice freedom—even if imperfect—for an unknown quantity. Or a belief that it is more difficult to develop one's full potential with demanding involvements. (Such reluctance is increasing with the recent consciousness-level-raising pronouncements of various feminist groups.)

5. An abiding distrust or resentment of men, due to personal observations of the disastrous course that relationships of women family members and friends have taken.

As for my special attention to the fulfillment of the neurotic needs of women, it should in no way suggest that I am unaware of the frailties of men, or the inequities confronting women on many fronts. It is simply that, as a woman, my understanding of the distaff side is more intimate and credible.

In the course of my research I have been impressed by the number of women who, notwithstanding the veritable path of destruction marking their dating and serious-relationship background, still attribute their incredible record to "circumstances beyond their control," or "just plain bad luck," thus absolving themselves of any real responsibility.

The "primary test" below is designed to show a pattern in your relationships that could reveal whether or not you may subconsciously want rejection or prefer to avoid any serious involvement.

1. Do girls with no more to offer than you invariably have more success with men?

2. At dinner parties, or on other occasions where everyone is in couples, are you usually the spare girl relegated to the stray man?

3. Does it always seem to be your "bad luck" to choose men who only want to use you (leaving when the privilege is revoked), or other obviously wrong-man types?

4. Upon learning that you have never been married, do most men appear surprised—at first?

5. Do "hot" prospects, panting to meet you at parties, usually cool to room, or even tundra, temperatures—or just plain melt into the thicket, not long after having had the "pleasure"?

6. "Just by chance," and though you are "blameless," do your affairs invariably end in bitter arguments?

7. Recently, have your announcements of newfound love or precipitously ended love affairs begun to evoke "What, again?" responses from friends and family alike?

8. Though you may look great on paper, causing friends to be forever fixing you up with blind dates, do they almost inevitably wind up in blind alleys?

9. Do you find that you often "inexplicably" lose interest in a man as soon as he becomes too attentive?

10. Do you neglect your personal appearance—carefully remaining fat, out of shape, or unkempt—to improve the possibility that you will be rejected by men?

If you "passed" this test, that is, answered three or more affirmatively, it is time to abandon all pretense and admit that, subconsciously at least, you do not *want* to get a man. Having admitted this, don't go into an immediate depression; on the contrary, you should begin to feel a sense of relief, and perhaps even a certain excitement. CONGRATU-LATIONS! YOU HAVE JUST TAKEN THE FIRST IMPORTANT STEP ALONG THE ROAD TO GREATER REJECTION FULFILL-MENT. Even if you scored two or less, do not feel automatically eliminated from participation in this program. The above test was simply indicative; only by carefully studying the entire book will you determine where you stand (or fall) neurotically.

Our second step involves organizing a well-coordinated program that assures maximum alienation and rejection. The effectiveness of this program, and its ultimate success, depends upon the proper selection of techniques, strategies, and attitudes best suited to your own case. (From this point on, you may feel free to think of yourself, *sans* guilt, as a "case".) In order to accomplish this, make choices based on:

1. Your natural inclinations.

2. Any area of special competence that you may have noticed during past processes of alienation.

3. Your most consistent compulsions.

4. The nature of the prospect in question.

5. The degree of rejection desired, and over what time period. (That is, whether you want to destroy a relationship so irreparably that not even a decent friendship

can be salvaged, or ruin it slowly for ongoing rejection gratification. There is much to be said for both.)

If you follow these simple guidelines while coordinating your program, you will soon find your potential for alienating men polished to a fine art, and all the rejection fulfillment I have promised—and you have longed for—yours to relish. In fact, as one of the world's foremost successful failures, I can personally guarantee that through your new program you will specifically enjoy:

1. A twenty-five-per-cent (minimum) increase in bittersweet, dateless Saturday nights and unmanned major holidays.

2. More and more deliciously frustrating, sleepless nights in which to ponder why "he" crossed the street against traffic, drove through a red light, or left the party by the side door to avoid speaking after the big date.

3. A fifty-per-cent (minimum) improvement in your ability to ferret out wrong-man prospects about whom you can whine and complain to friends (for those of you who believe misery is best when shared).

4. Increased frustration opportunities thanks to waiting for "no shows." (Benefits here will include shorter fingernails; reluctance to remove makeup at ten o'clock even though "he" was expected at seven; concern that he phoned while you were in the shower; repeated calls to the operator to check if your line is working, etc. Added fringe benefit: crying yourself to sleep.)

5. A satisfying dire prognosis for affairs that appear ongoing (including futureless marriages, should they occur through some oversight).

6. A miserably happy-ever-after life of stormy confrontations, in cases where relationships endure in spite of all efforts.

But it is time to move from promises and generalities to specifics, to what I term "Basic Alienating Procedures," or BAP.

Basic Alienating Procedures: The Nine Vital Primers*

The foundation of any master plan for alienating men and assuring greater rejection fulfillment is to select the appropriate basic attitude, or primer.

Following is a selection of primers I have found to be most effective, suggestions of how to apply them, and a few examples of how others have used them to good effect.

---

* Primer, incidentally, is pronounced "pry-mer" and is here used in the sense of preparation for setting things in motion, as in "priming the rejection pump."

Primer #1:
The Always-See-or-Suspect-the-Worst Attitude
(The Eternal Pessimist)

If you think of the five people you like least or find most worthy of rejection, chances are at least one would be an eternal pessimist. For these doomsayers, who never have anything good to say about anyone—often including themselves—cast a pall of gloom wherever they go. If you study such types for pointers, it could help considerably in the development of your own always-see-or-suspect-the-worst attitude.

My own candidate is a particularly beautiful and successful failure, a former co-worker I shall call Sally. An hour at lunch with her sufficed to depress anyone for the remainder of the week. Not surprisingly, she was studiously avoided or constantly rejected by men (and women). However, having already begun my research into successful-failure techniques, I spoke with her often, though even for a seasoned failure researcher like me, her always critical, always complaining conversation soon wore heavy.

As you might suspect, much of her discourse centered around her distressing and "incomprehensible" lack of success with men. Yet I noticed that no matter what man she met or discussed, she invariably mentioned four or five shortcomings or blemishes for every grudgingly acknowledged asset. And if, in rare instances, no defects were immediately visible, she became very suspicious, naturally *suspecting* the worst.

Sally also kept a complete and unexpurgated record on who was splitting up with whom and why, among the famous, near-famous, and not famous at all. She apparently scoured the papers and magazines that dealt with such tidbits. She was a recognized repository of gossip, not only for the usual whispered scandals but also for an assortment of exclusives. "You know that sweet, married, all-American actress? Well, she's actually a lesbian! . . . And the great macho male actor? He was once a male prostitute, on Forty-second Street, no less!" Her inventory, replete with names and dates, could match, entry for entry, the Guinness Book of World Records.

I soon got the feeling that hearing derogatory news about someone else, particularly anyone who seemed happy, provided her with a kind of "mouth to mouth" resuscitation.

To help reinforce her always-see-or-suspect-the-worst attitude, she kept a handy supply of statistics on divorce and the number of women abandoned with children, plus the latest reports on how most marriages that did last were held together only for religious, economic, or business reasons, or for the children.

All ASSW types I have studied have the ability to filter out the good and zero in on the negative. Concentrating on the dismal and dark side, we will soon begin to see ourselves, and life in general, in an unfavorable light, making it increasingly easy to see the worst in everyone. If you think that you have a predisposition toward this attitude, by all means choose this Primer #1 and develop it to perfection. Vital here is your PF, or Predisposition Factor, that is, making proper snap or slower judgments.

Snap Judgments

Experience has proved that the sooner you can formulate an unfavorable impression of anyone, the better. If you dally, there is always the danger you may become confused and think you detect positive qualities among the dross. Besides, why take a week or a month to form a negative impression when you can do it in a few minutes?

To make an effective snap judgment, briefly analyze the next man you meet and immediately place him in some category. For example, decide that he is the quiet, rather reserved type. Having done this, think of all the things wrong with any such person, dredging up anything from clichés and stereotypes to unfounded rumors or admonitions that Grandma used to make to buttress your conclusions.

Decide that the quiet ones cannot be trusted; you never know what they are thinking; still water runs deep and dirty. (Remember the dirty deal you got from What's His Name, who seemed so nice and quiet at first?) Besides, the reserved ones are usually "uptight" and have a communication problem, are poor mixers, and are no fun to be with.

Of course, when you meet someone who is outgoing, extroverted, and seemingly affable, you cannot afford to be any less vigilant. Beware: the talkative ones are often trying to "sell you a bill of goods." And their self-confidence is frequently offensive, especially when, as everyone knows, it is only a subterfuge to cover up their inferiority. Decide, too, that if he talks a lot he's probably lying half the time (only half?), is interested only in himself, and probably says the same thing to all the girls.

Slower Judgments

If you meet someone difficult to categorize immediately, keep scrutinizing him until you do ferret out the worst; remember, it is there, if only you know where to look for it. Examine him critically to find fault with the way he dresses. Maybe he fails to look you in the eye (or, conversely, stares at you); doesn't have a sufficiently firm handshake (or, conversely, holds your hand *too* tight); appears too forward (or acts as though he isn't sure enough of himself). One way or another, you'll find something.

After you've found some bad character traits—and who, after all, is perfect?—you may think you're on safe rejection ground. Don't: you're simply off on the right foot. All sorts of pitfalls lie ahead. Here, like signs on a narrow, winding road, are some things to remember:

• If someone is generous, he probably only wants to obligate you later; after all, no one does anything for nothing.

• If someone has not made a pass at you after the first few dates, there is probably something amiss in the masculinity department (but it is also well known that if someone is too aggressive, he is doubtless only trying to prove something).

• Although a handsome prospect may seem unassuming and sincere, ninety-nine per cent of the time he is actually vain and self-centered, and will eventually prove fickle.

• Beware of any man who smiles at you—he may be the currently sought rapist-strangler plaguing the area.

• Suspect that the attractive, friendly fellow who lives in your block and rides the bus with you irregularly is probably not gainfully employed. (Try to check what section of the paper he is reading, and don't be surprised if it's the want ads, especially if he looks neat and well groomed. Or if he rides regularly at an early hour, suspect that his is a nondescript job.)

• Tense up perceptibly any time a man invites you to visit a friend (probably there is a prearranged plan for the friend to disappear as soon as you are settled). Or question him as if he were a suspected felon if he invites you to take part in any activity outside the city limits. Refuse to remove your coat if you visit his house; in fact, wrap it more tightly around you. Say that you are comfortable only on the narrowest chair or hassock-for-one in the room.

• Always try to catch him in a lie. Never be so naive as to accept at face value any reason offered for being late, breaking a date, or having limited funds. First, it's probably a damn lie. Second, even if the facts are true, the motives are doubtless ulterior.

• If he claims to have a prestigious job, ask him a few discreet questions to try to prove otherwise. If this fails, call his office and question his co-workers or friends, asking them not to tell that you called (one of them invariably will).

• If he claims he's divorced, have a lawyer friend check; or when you are at his house slyly rearrange sofa pillows or examine the medicine chest to try to establish the feminine presence he may deny. In the event you don't have access to his home, try to get at the truth by looking through his wallet while he's out of the room.

• Above all, use your imagination and ingenuity. If you honestly suspect the worst in anyone, you can almost invariably find it.

I cannot emphasize too strongly the importance of Primer #1. It probably accounts for a greater percentage of rejection fulfillment than any other. In case you yourself have moments of optimism or are feeling "up," quickly remind yourself that even the silverest cloud must have a dark lining. But you have to look for it.

Primer #2:
The Contrary Base

This primer is in some ways similar to Primer #1 and is often used in conjunction with it by above-average successful-failure artisans. With the Contrary Base, however, it is not essential always to see the worst, though it helps! The only definite requirement here is that you prime yourself to be *out* of step and *in* disagreement with everyone and everything as often as possible.

Basic here is to convince yourself that you are only trying to be honest. After all, honesty is as respected as motherhood. Decide, too, that you will get more attention and be more stimulating if you do not conform sheeplike like everyone else. Add to this the fact that to have a mind of one's own is capital, that you will seem more intelligent if you point out things no one else observed, that what some may term "hard to please" you call "being your own person."

Let's take an example: The next time someone calls to invite you out, make yourself available only at times when your caller is not, particularly if his prior engagement involves some important business meeting or dinner with his recently widowed mother. If he begins to explain why he can't switch or postpone, say, "It's up to you." Or if he finally agrees to the day you demand and suggests an hour, always try to have it changed. If he suggests seven, explain, "I won't be free till eight," thereby implying you have a date beforehand. If you sense you are having an effect, add, "I must be home no later than ten-thirty." If he's at all suspicious he'll immediately suspect you have a late date. I've known this to drive men mad—or at least out the door.

If you live in the suburbs, no matter how difficult your house may be to find or how early your date, refuse his suggestion that you meet in the city. If for any reason he would prefer to pick you up, and your house is conveniently located, insist on meeting him out. If he's at all neurotic himself—and if he isn't at this point, he soon will be—he'll probably think you don't want him to meet your parents or roommates.

On the night of your date, if he asks where you'd like to go, ask him for suggestions; then quietly reject them one by one. Always be vague about your objections, so that he won't have any concrete guidelines to use when trying to choose a place more to your liking. When he arrives at the "Oh!-I-know-the-perfect-place-why-didn't-I-think-of-it-before" point, backtrack and say you would prefer to go to one of the places already rejected, and about which you are obviously not enthusiastic.

If any parking problem is encountered when you are out with someone, always act as if you thought that he had deliberately arranged it. After refusing to be let out in front of wherever you are going, complain all during the long walk back. Mumble about the hard day you had at the office. Say, "If you'd warned me, I would have brought along my walking shoes."

Any time he takes you visiting, demonstrate that you are incapable of being entertained. Decline anything offered and request something not available. Always dislike the music everyone else seems to be enjoying. If everyone is raving about a play that has received great critical acclaim, say how much you hated it. (Conversely, if everyone is talking about how lousy something was, say, "Really? I found it very sensitive . . . very moving." The implication that others' sensitivity is deficient is especially productive.) You can apply the same tactic at the movies or the theater. If everyone seems to be enjoying the performance, pick it apart at every opportunity—ridiculing the actors, direction, plot, etc. (loud enough for those around you to hear). Or if everyone else appears bored, laugh pointedly, saying, "This playwright is really subtle, isn't he?" In any group or party situation, if everyone decides to play cards or some other game, decline to join them, but kibitz openly, commenting on the way everyone plays. Or suggest another activity altogether, and if the group demurs, sit off to one side, sulking. If your date seems to be having a good time in spite of all your efforts, develop a headache at the height of his fun and insist that he take you home. Immediately.

If your date is fond of the friends he has taken you to see, perhaps having told you that they were very attractive or special in some way, seize the first opportunity to run them down. Single out those you know he especially likes (and probably wants *you* to like), saying, "Is George really all that bright?" Or, "I thought you said Suzy was pretty!"

Be sure to take issue with any important decision he has made, such as a planned European vacation. ("In view of the balance of payments problem and our trade deficit, isn't that rather selfish?") However, if he limited his vacation to the States, make it clear that you consider him provincial and lacking in imagination.

If you have some tangible good points, some men may try to overlook your contrary base or primer, considering you simply "difficult." But after you have learned and applied more advanced techniques, such as those discussed later in "The Argument Arsenal" and "The Last Supper (Out)," they will realize that the problem is more serious. Consequently, as you receive more and more rejections, you will, though subconsciously gratified, be consciously more bitter . . . which in turn will make you all the more contrary: the snowball effect.

I trust that at this point you are already beginning to see the importance of building, of having a coordinated program rather than leaving your neurotic behavior to chance or fate.

Primer #3:
Having a
Love Affair
with Oneself

It is common knowledge that all the world loves a lover; and without some self-love no one could survive. Even so, when properly applied this primer will enable you to give the impression that your self-love is so intense no one else need apply. It will make potential rivals quickly yield, assuring the rejection you so deeply desire.

The key words here are: self-praise, self-love, and self-aggrandizement, the "keyest" word of all, of course, being "self."

As I take inventory of the vainest people I know, I become convinced that those who display the most self-adulation in public are the least deserving. Conspicuous in this category is a former disc jockey, now on TV, whose love affair with himself is of gargantuan proportions. And while I have opted to limit myself to the feminine neurotic gender in this book, this man's case is so classic I feel it must be included. Though you may not be able to use his conduct as an exact pattern, you can consider this as a preview of wrong-man types.

If I were to describe my friend, I would say that he was a ladies' man, mainly because I know that's how he sees himself. Indeed, whenever he is seen at smart gallery openings, chic restaurants, and other places where luminaries hold forth and gossip columnists gather, it is usually with a four-star, banner-type girl. (He tells his wife it's all in a day's work.) On other occasions, if ever he is without a

girl, it is not for lack of trying, since he regularly proposi-
tions everything mobile.

Around the office, where he is affectionately known as
"the prick," his conversation consists mainly of his relat-
ing how he "scored" with this one or that—not excluding
some rather well-known women—or whom he would like
to make out with. The balance of his verbal treasures is
dedicated to putting the touch on fellow employees, to
help maintain the style of living he deserves but cannot
always afford.

When I first met him some years ago, he was employed
by a small radio station. Fifteen minutes into the conversation, however, he had already confided what a great success his show was, how many letters and calls he received
from women literally throwing themselves at him, and the
kind of car he drove. In addition, he had dropped the
names of several famous people who were "close personal
friends." (Practically any woman he mentioned was or had
been an "intimate friend," and without much prodding he
would share virtually any secrets such friendships could
produce.)

On cue at the end of his self-eulogy, he offered me the
opportunity to leave the party with him to go "someplace
where we could talk." Translated, it was clear that meant
someplace where he could continue his self-aggrandizing
monologue, notch his gun with me, and continue on to the
next moving target. As it happened, I was not in the market for that particular brand of rejection, so we became
"friends" instead.

Of course, taste and neurotic need cannot be dictated,
and a girl friend of mine, antenna high for just such a
wrong-man type, tuned in to his wavelength practically
on sight. But, according to her account, their frequency
compatibility ended in bed: she swears he is the worst
lover not only in the Continental United States but
throughout the world (her experience is broad). According
to her, the Sex Machine (self-proclaimed) could be

"charged" only with great difficulty, operated briefly, and featured a "switch" of quite inadequate proportions. And so we come to the reason behind the attitude of many of those who flaunt love affairs with themselves. Often it is to overcome some sense of inadequacy and to convince themselves and others that they are worthy in spite of these shortcomings.

I think of another example, a stunning model frequently rhapsodized over in newspapers and magazines who keeps her conversation egocentrically focused on her perfect attributes and many exploits in order to divert attention from her lack of education and her inability to discuss anything else. The only multisyllable word I ever heard her use was "mascara."

Nonetheless, we cannot overlook the fact that some people are genuinely and faithfully in love with themselves for one simple reason, which can be expressed in three words: I'm so wonderful. If you plan to use this primer, certain general rules of procedures apply:

• Always make "I" the subject, "me" the object, and "my" the possessive of as many sentences as possible.

• Include an abundance of details on your success professionally, whatever your field. (If it is based on your supreme beauty, the more frivolous the conversation, the better. For example, talk about the quandary you were in while trying to select a dress earlier that evening—one set your hair off so beautifully but another seemed to "bring out" your eyes. You might also point out how your eyes change color according to the shades of your clothes, your mood, etc.).

• Whenever anyone else tries to speak about himself, cut him down to size forthwith with an account of how you, or someone you know well, did the same thing better.

• Consider only your own comfort and convenience, no matter how others are inconvenienced.

• If unavoidable circumstances force you to subject

yourself to public transportation, or to companions of less lofty stature than usual, or to any but the finest restaurants, make it clear that you are playing the game under protest.

• If in certain gracious moments you feel a trifle self-conscious about your degree of perfection, admit to such character faults as being too good, too generous, or too honest. (But never be too self-conscious to make "flat out" statements like, "I've always been very smart," or "People always tell me I'm beautiful.")

• Never be shy about public displays of affection based on your beauty. Like anyone truly in love, never miss an opportunity to catch fleeting glances of your beloved as you pass mirrors, shop windows, or any surface that reflects your gorgeous image. Another excellent time for prolonged mirror-study and self-admiration is when someone is standing by to take you out, especially when you are already late.

When there are no mirrors available, make your obsession with your image apparent by affecting various of the following mannerisms and expressions as the circumstances and your personality suggest:

1. The cutie-pie pucker pout.
2. The wide-eyed baby-doll stare.
3. The one-raised-eyebrow *très-sophistiqué* look.
4. The dramatic sweeping back of hair, carefully coiffed earlier to tumble into your face.
5. The breathy I-am-a-sex-symbol voice.
6. The profile (or best-angle) picture-perfect pose.
7. The "on stage" affected laugh.
8. The broad "A," or any assumed accent (when you remember).

In public places, find things to do that require you to walk around often, so that audiences there can be treated to an unobstructed view. When you return to your escort, call attention to the "stir" you created. Say, "Did you see every man's head turn as I crossed the room? Men are really so gross!" Or in a spirit of basic if false modesty and an I-am-too-humble-for-the-idolatry-that-is-constantly-showered-on-me attitude, ask him why people stare at you so much. Try to get his opinion as to why compliments are so often given to you. Say, "Why do you think George, that handsome young V.P. in the office, you know the one, keeps telling me I'm the most perfect creature he's ever met?"

• Make it a practice to run down the appearance of any other attractive girls in your group, office, or even on the silver screen. Give a feature-by-feature analysis: fat legs, buck teeth, big mouth, short neck, circles under the eyes, etc. Comment that it looks as if this or that one had a nose job, or a face lift. Later, subtly call attention to your natural, more regular features. At this point it is a good idea to add, "Not that I am conceited," because he might not have noticed.

• If someone is reticent about giving compliments, begin to complain about your best feature. If you are wasp-waisted, say what a terrible time you have finding slacks to fit because your waist is only 21. Or tell how your eyelashes are "terrible," so long they constantly get in your eyes. Any comment he makes in response to such "complaints" is almost sure to be the sought-after compliment.

• In general, whenever anyone gives you a compliment, milk it to the last drop. "Do you really like my hair?" running your fingers through it. "You know, a lot of people, even my hairdresser at first, think the lighter streaks are bleached, but they're all mine. When I was little, everyone on my block used to marvel at it, and in the summer when I get tan and the streaks are still lighter, you can imagine." The possibilities are virtually endless.

Finally, no matter how desirable you may otherwise be, any interested man will realize that, in matters of love, two's company but three's a crowd and bow out, leaving you a beautiful and gratified rejectee.

Primer #4:
The Big
Self-Put-Down

Many of you, while yearning for the degree of rejection fulfillment that the having-an-affair-with-oneself attitude could obviously produce, may nevertheless feel too self-conscious or "modest" to develop it properly for yourself. If so, you may feel much more comfortable using the opposite approach, the purpose of which is to convince all prospects that you are so unworthy you do not even like yourself. Equipped with such an attitude, you should soon make it apparent to all prospects that only the most tasteless, unaware, desperate, and/or crazy person could possibly like you.

When preparing this primer, keep on reminding yourself how obnoxious you have always found all conceited and self-centered people. Also, dismissing any favorable remarks that people have made about you as insincere or idle flattery, concentrate on any criticism that you have received and any imperfections you may have. Frequently think about people who have done something you would like to have done and constantly compare yourself with them. Tell yourself that even if you tried to accept a compliment gracefully, the giver would soon discover it was undeserved, proving an embarrassment to both of you. However, from time to time, just to give yourself a little self-esteem, think about some small success you have had, or of someone even worse off than you. But if this begins to be too heady a sensation, think how someone generally worse off than you is, in some way, more successful.

In putting yourself down, call attention to your worst

defects, make derogatory jokes about yourself, and in general prosecute the case against yourself. For example, the next time someone says you look nice, even if only in passing, explain how old your dress is, how everyone hates you in that color, and that the only reason you are wearing it is because it has long sleeves and you think you are catching cold. (Expanding on the latter, at that moment or later, you can use it as an excuse for why your skin looks so dry, or in general why you look so poorly.)

If a woman compliments you in the presence of your prospect, tell her you bought the coat, dress, or whatever in some bargain basement—and tell her she will find racks of them if she goes there. Show her, however, how it hikes up in the back, and how you have to keep the collar pinned in because it is so ugly. If you got a great buy on some garment because it had a spot or imperfection, be sure to point it out, even as you adore pointing blemishes out on your person.

If someone compliments you on a new hair style, explain that you only wear it that way because you have a thin spot on one side (or better, because of your bald spot). Or confess that your sister says you look like an old maid when you wear your hair that way, because all the fashion magazines are featuring shorter (or longer) cuts this year.

By no means limit your self-put-down to your appearance. For instance, never let a whole evening pass without letting the prospect know how many mistakes you always seem to make on your job, how all your sisters are much prettier than you are, what a miserable time you had in school (working in if possible the fact that you were never invited to the proms, or always had to date the ugliest boy in town).

In addition, don't fail to mention recent evidence that indicates things have not improved. For instance, you might confide in him how a sexy girl friend always seems to attract your men away from you, and sigh and say how much you wished you looked like her. Tell him how often you are alone on New Year's Eve. Also, of vital importance: if you have ever been left in the lurch, or better yet at the church, share this experience with him in all its heart-rending detail.

You can apply the BSPD more easily, I have found, if you tell yourself that you are simply trying to win his sympathy, or allow him to build his ego by feeling superior to you. Deep down, of course, you know that while people contribute to charities they seldom go to them for entertainment, and that no one's ego can be elevated by winning an unwanted, or discarded, uncontested prize.

If, as I hope, you are by this point keeping a notebook in which you jot those points and primers that seem especially applicable to you, I urge you, if Primer #4 applies, to inscribe, in bold or even capital letters, the following: "If you stamp yourself REJECT, DISCARD, INFERIOR, NULL & VOID, the message will not be lost."

Primer #5:
The Walk-on-Me
Doormat Conditioner

At first glance this primer might be confused with the one just offered. However, while the two can be used to complement each other for complete lackluster, the previous primer is intended mainly to get you used to accepting compliments ungracefully and belittling yourself verbally. This primer takes things much farther: it is a concentrate of pure masochism meant to make you thrive on mistreatment. Meanwhile as you lie prone letting a person who uses you at his convenience, wiping his feet on you, more suitable prospects come and go, completely turned off.

An attractive and otherwise intelligent friend of mine typifies this attitude in a fairly refined form. After a six-year affair with a married policeman, during which my friend had to defer to his wife on holidays and all important occasions, and at gift-giving times usually received only an apology or explanation, he finally got a divorce. But—a thousand arguments, countless humiliations, and two abortions after their first meeting—he kept his divorce a closely guarded secret; it was almost a year before she found out. Meanwhile, still using his nonexistent wife as an excuse, he started going out with other girls. When caught, he said to her, "I'm a free man," and, "You're beginning to sound like my wife."

Of course, every so often a drop of honey drips into the vinegar, and he declares that he does care for and want her (he avoids any use of the word "love").

The other side of this dubious coin is that her policeman is insanely jealous of her if ever she dares look at another man. But my friend, far from reacting negatively, considers his jealousy a good sign, for doesn't it prove after all that she's really the one? Or so she maintains between crying spells.

Between the crying spells and bitter complaints about this obviously untenable situation, my friend makes excuses for her beloved boy in blue based on his crazy, mixed-up childhood; disappointment at finding his wife had been unfaithful; frustration at his failure to make sergeant, and similar grounds. Besides, she reasons, "having" him is better than having no one at all; and if she gives up now, she will have invested six years for nothing. (Ten years for nothing would be more palatable, presumably.)

I could make excuses for my friend, but I won't because I know that deep down, and in spite of the somewhat drawn expression she is beginning to show, she must be enjoying the years of rejection that she has voluntarily accepted. (Incidentally, she has admitted that her involvement is more out of a sense of challenge than love.)

In later sections—"Ferreting Out the Wrong Man," "The High-Risk-Sex Co-Star," etc.—we will advise further on how to orient yourself toward the exploitative, inconsiderate men who clearly don't care anything about you, and who are an essential part of Primer #5. If you are already into such a situation, remember my friend's rationale for continuing the relationship, discouraging remarks by family and friends notwithstanding. Bear in mind that you are the best judge of what diet best feeds your own neurosis, and you have just as much right to rejection fulfillment as anyone else.

Primer #6: The Women's Liberation Gloss

"Up with all powerful sisterhood, down with all men, so oppressive; under a banner of hostile extremes, we can be twice as aggressive." —J.K.

While most women, and even men, *au courant* with the issues of Women's Liberation, are recognizing more and more the validity of many feminist grievances, the positions and attitudes of certain factions seem calculated mainly to alienate men. This movement provides a built-in nationwide primer that was totally unavailable to us only a few short years ago. Needless to say, the possibilities should be fully exploited.

The idea here is to find a Women's Liberation group that has largely abandoned the political aspect of the struggle (concern for better job and promotional opportunities; day-care facilities; credit rights; a more realistic, flexible definition of the role of the sexes, etc.) in order to rail and rant against *all* men and advance the most bizarre theories possible. If you enter such a group with a basic resentment against men, by the time your consciousness level has been elevated by the rhetoric, you will be so hostile toward them you will invite immediate rejection. At this point, convinced that men are unworthy in any case, you can pretend not to feel frustrated by the rebuffs that you experience, and relax and luxuriate in the gratification they provide.

Once you have chosen the group most responsive to and compatible with your particular needs and inclinations, you will formulate your own rules to keep your desirably negative attitude intact. However, to give you some idea of the many possibilities this primer offers, following are Nine Commandments you can use as guidelines.

Nine Commandments for Alienating Men— Women's Liberation Style

1. Cultivate the habit of applying the expression "male chauvinist pig" indiscriminately to all men (even those who are sympathetic to the movement). Consider all men in terms of those who have deceived, raped, and otherwise abused women.

2. On a date with an apparent nonchauvinist, advance the most radical positions possible, such as, "Male surgeons take obvious sadistic delight in maiming their female patients." If he takes issue, mentally label him narrow-minded and unworthy of any more of your time.

3. Bone up on inconsequential "evidence" that proves women are oppressed (aren't hurricanes named after women?) and interject it into all conversations, no matter how unrelated.

4. Vociferously demand equality in all areas unless it is not in your interest (matters of alimony, paying the checks, combat service, etc.).

5. Once convinced that men are the oppressor class, try to emulate them in every way possible. (Act "aggressive," "competitive," "exploitative," etc.)

6. Constantly squabble with and snipe at more popular or attractive WL figures, while protesting the jealous, petty, unreasonable stereotype attributed to women.

7. Using Glorious Gloria Steinem as model, resolve to resist the repression of restrictive girdles and confining bras. (Flip and flop about, disregarding entirely any possible differences between your figure and hers.) Moreover, and though there may be no apparent clear and present danger, wear the most ill-fitting clothes and unstylish hair

styles to preclude the remote possibility that you will be mistaken for a sex object.

8. When talking of or referring to Women's Liberation, assume the dour look and grimly serious expression you do for funerals and catastrophes. Completely abandon your sense of humor (and demand that everyone else do likewise).

9. If a man shows the slightest interest in you, break him in right. Invite him home, then suggest that he get the apron behind the door and cook dinner while you watch TV. If he complies, have him wash the dishes. If he does that, ask him to mop the floor. If again he does as you bid, you're in trouble. But not really; for obviously the guy's a creep, a sissy, probably a masochist to boot. After he's finished mopping, put him to the test. Say, "I suppose now you'd like to try on one of my dresses!" If he demurs, tell him you knew he was an MCP all along. If he accepts, you're obviously dealing with someone whose neurosis is even greater than yours. As you throw him out, scream, "Pervert!" or some other likely epithet.

Primer #7:
The Know-It-All
(Walking Encyclopedia)

*"As a walking encyclopedia, you
will be out of place off a shelf."*
—J.K.

In order to bring out the full obnoxious brilliance of this attitude, you should begin with a very good mind, great intellectual curiosity, and exceptional retentive powers. Moreover, you should always try to know as much as you can about as many subjects as possible.

Of course, you may be thinking, this should only make you a more interesting person and stimulating conversationalist. However, the idea behind the know-it-all (walking encyclopedia) primer is to exhibit your knowledge in such a way as to make others feel inferior or uninformed— "others" being a general category that includes practically everyone.

When you have perfected this superior attitude, you probably will, like the heavy, cumbersome book you resemble, spend most of your time on the shelf. For while you may sometimes be sought out for information, who would want to settle down for an evening's entertainment with an encyclopedia? Small wonder so many rejection seekers can be found in the know-it-all category.

One genuine KIA(WE) I know comes in the smartly attractive form of a woman of about thirty-five named Sharon. She is without doubt one of the brightest people I have ever met. No matter what is under discussion, she knows (at least) three times more about it than anyone else present. And no matter what project may be planned, she knows ten ways to do it better (five of which would prove everyone else wrong).

If anyone makes the mistake of asking her about, or even mentioning, a city, he or she is likely to be treated to an extended travelogue about it. But Sharon doesn't spend all her time talking; she also listens, critically, to everyone's conversation, waiting to pounce on misinformation, errors of fact, improper use of words, or grammar. Her detailed corrections are in the clear tone of the class smart aleck (remember him, or her?). Sharon never hesitates to take issue with any incorrect report on radio or TV, and as she superimposes her corrected version of what transpired, she is vaguely condescending to anyone who naively prefers the official version. She carefully proofreads newspapers and magazines for typographical and other errors, to demonstrate how much more competent she is than their staffs. She knows more about symptoms, operations, or rare diseases than anyone, including the person suffering from them, not to mention his or her doctor. Sharon is never shy with legal advice and rarely hesitates to overrule any judicial decision (not excluding some by the Supreme Court).

Once when a friend arrived unannounced from out of town, I made the neurotic mistake of asking Sharon along with us, when I could find no other friend free for the evening. Predictably, she wasted no time getting into character.

At the French restaurant we went to, she insisted on communicating with the waiter in French, though it appeared that his English was far better than her French. Nor did she hesitate to countermand my friend's orders: the wine should *not* be chilled but served at room temperature, and of course a white wine was indicated (this was established in front of the wine steward).

In general, the evening was a disaster, its one redeeming feature being that for that brief span of time I felt perfectly well adjusted by comparison.

However, as I look back to my first meeting with Sharon in college, though she was even then outstanding and always head of the class, she was much less arrogantly brilliant. In fact, in those days she got along reasonably well with men, and even had a sense of humor.

Her specific romantic interest at that time was a highly eligible graduate-school student who planned to go into the foreign service. Though Sharon seemed to enjoy his company, whenever the question of marriage came up her whole attitude changed. In fact, in a moment of candor she told me she did not want to abandon her own plans for an exciting career in advertising to retire to some faraway place, to play a supporting role to someone whose work didn't really interest her.

When her affair with him started to cool, she seemed more reluctant to become involved in serious relations with men and more interested in realizing her full intellectual potential. But, though I am sure she knew even then that she was not interested in marriage before reaching certain goals, she was too steeped in the every-woman-has-to-get-a-man tradition of our times to acknowledge it and act accordingly. So she continued to date, as if hoping for a meaningful involvement, meanwhile cultivating more and more her know-it-all (walking encyclopedia) primer.

As time went on, her aggressive attitude began to affect all her relationships, and when she finally landed her dream job in advertising, she knew far better than her clients what they wanted, and her authoritative manner did not endear her to her fellow workers either. She lost job after job, and, disenchanted, she tried teaching. Though I would have thought this might well be her calling (since she maintained a pedantic I-am-the-teacher-you-are-the-student attitude with everyone), it did not work out. Even with teachers, apparently, there's a point of diminishing returns in knowing-it-all.

As Sharon's professional life withered, her relationships

with men went from bad to worse. To fill the growing vacuum in her life, she redoubled her efforts in research, knowledge-gathering, and criticism, which she bestowed ever more freely on an ever-shrinking audience.

Buffing Up Your Know-It-All Attitude and Image

As you put the finishing touches on your own KIA(WE) attitude, convince yourself that all you really want is to be well informed and to get the respect you deserve. (After all, you wouldn't want the man you may become interested in to think you were a birdbrain.) Tell yourself, too, that an intelligent, secure man wants a bright, stimulating woman. (Why, after all, should a woman defer intellectually to a man and pretend to be less bright than she actually is?)

Once this is established, begin using as many of Sharon's tactics as you can. Don't be reluctant to introduce controversial subjects that may have confounded the experts for years, complete with definitive no-nonsense answers supplying the *real* truth.

Between times, when you have no dates or eligible prospects around to impress—which will become more and more frequent as you develop this attitude and put it into practice—keep sharp by bossing sales people around and setting public servants and the like straight.

Even if you have no children, be generous in your advice to those who do, telling them how to bring them up. Make a specialty of furnishing free, and preferably unsolicited, advice to women about how to solve problems with their husbands or mates, though you may have neither.

Your reading material should always include little-known books on universal theories, as well as on esoteric and technical subjects. Whenever you have an audience, even of one, slip references from these tomes into the conversation. Show surprise that no one else is familiar with them. For instance, if the subject of pollution comes up, as it will sooner or later if you live in any urban environment, say, "Did you know that in the Ginza—Tokyo's main drag, if you're not familiar with the Orient—there's an electronic sign giving air-pollution readings for sulphur dioxide and carbon monoxide, in parts per million?" Chances are that not one rejection target in a million will either know it or be able to top it.

When currently popular authors are discussed, always downgrade the work that made them famous. Denounce this popular work as too commercial, unimaginative, replete with clichés and unoriginal ideas and designed to appeal to only the most pedestrian tastes. Whenever possible, compare the famous work to an obscure one by the same author, finding the latter far superior. Also—a very important point—in these and other conversations, always remember never to use a monosyllabic word when a longer one will do. For example: never "settle" when you can "adjudicate"; never "eat food" when you can "consume comestibles"; never "feel lust" when you can "experience concupiscence," "want" when you can "be desirous of," "lack" when you can "have a paucity of," be "bad" when you can be "nefarious," be "sinful" when you can be "peccant"—the possibilities are endless.

Refer to authors by their last names only, particularly when asking questions: "What did you think of Schwartz on composition?" or "Do you agree with Luria on algae?"

Gather and commit to memory odd bits of information no one else is likely to know, and work them in when related or remotely related subjects are under discussion. For instance, when Australian tennis is being discussed, you need not be just one of many who comment on an Aussie player's backhand or topspin; you will be able to point out that in Australia over a million square miles of the territory are uninhabitable. Or you might give a short—or even long—discourse on the curious phenomenon of the boomerang.

If perchance anyone invites you out, line up a list of lectures, seminars, and documentary films you would like to see. Afterward, review the entire proceeding, adding whenever you can something that should have been included, and refuting fallacious statements. For lighter entertainment, ask him to take you to a museum early, and stay late. Be so completely enthralled with the paintings or *objets d'art* (*never* forget the value of foreign words sprinkled like salt throughout your conversational *ragoût*) that all your conversation centers around the origin of certain articles and the biographies of their creators.

If your walking target endures this, test his patience even further by inviting him to join you in university seminars on some involved, highly technical subject, unrelated to anything he is remotely interested in. If even this fails to deter him, present him some massive and weighty volumes, then interrogate him as to their contents, preferably only a day or two after he has received them. In all likelihood he will not have even dipped into them, so your task of tripping him up should not be too hard. When you catch him, say (coldly), "I can see you're not serious about me."

On a quiet evening at home, if he appears to be getting romantic, begin jabbering about ancient religious doctrines, comparative Eastern cultures, or other equally fascinating subjects. Or, read him some fourteenth-century poetry, preferably in Old English. This should make his evening with you as romantic and exciting as holding hands with a weighty reference book.

Primer #8:
The Big Lie

"Never tell the truth if a lie is possible."
—J.K.

Basic to this primer is the following truth: The more fundamental and meaningful the lies you choose to tell about yourself, the better. While exaggerations and white lies can serve as attractive curlicues, the essential lies must be about something deep-rooted in you. You can, for example, lie about your religion, change your name, and reconstruct an entirely new family tree. Or you may lie about your marital status—claiming to be single and practically a virgin though you actually are separated from your husband in another town where you have left two children with his mother. Or, conversely, if you are and always have been single but think it sounds more provocative to claim that you have been married, by all means invent an ex-husband.

Suppose, for instance, you are secretary to an executive in a large, prestigious firm. Appropriate the executive's title, claim a tripled salary, and purport to have a secretary of your own. You also might want to invent a suitably impressive educational or professional background. A practical bit of advice, should you choose this approach, is the absolute necessity to save money: try missing meals, carrying cheese sandwiches from home for lunch, washing your own hair, getting a second job, etc. With the money thus saved, invest in a super apartment, flashy foreign car, and other accoutrements of conspicuous consumption. If asked, pretend you come from a wealthy family, bought the right stock at the right time, or were remembered in someone's will. With this approach, you might fall into the trap of thinking you are trying to attract someone with money, but actually your time should be devoted to men who seem primarily interested in the money you don't have.

Other lies you might consider telling about yourself: claim your hair color is natural though it is dyed; pretend you love housework or are a great cook (when actually you have ordered dinner for two sent up from a chic restaurant); claim you are politically liberal when you are an archconservative. Singly, each may not prove totally self-destructive, but the collective impact over a sustained period can be devastating.

The number-one all-time-champion, consummate-liar-of-her-time award goes to an actress friend of mine who constantly typecast herself in liar roles. She sheathed herself in such a veneer of lies that when a friend of hers talked to me about her recently I didn't even know whom he was referring to. That is no small feat when you consider that I have known her for over ten years and had spoken to her a scant five days before.

Not that I was unaccustomed to her constant claiming that she had just been chosen to star in some "fan-*tas*-tic" production (which never materialized), spent the weekend in Vegas with such-and-such world-famous producer, or was planning a world cruise on a rich industrialist's yacht. What fooled me was that for my friend she had exoticized her last name, claimed she was French and begun speaking English with a French accent, though she did not speak a word of French, and revealed to one and all that she had left her husband back in Paris, though she has never married—not surprisingly.

As my informant went on and on about this long-time friend of mine whom he had met and been impressed by (on totally false pretenses), the more confused I became. Only after he mentioned her latest movie, in which she played the ex-girl friend of the leading man (in fact, a prostitute with whom he slept in a flashback), and after cross-checking her address with him, did I recognize my friend the actress—charming liar, successful failure. And though at the time I thought I covered my own mixed-up tracks rather skillfully, the truth about her did out before long. The next time I saw her formerly fascinated pursuer, he couldn't stop saying how synthetic and "sick" she was . . . and what a big liar.

I reminded him that she hurt no one, might only have been teasing him or practicing, since she constantly has to assume other roles. Fortunately for her and her desire for rejection fulfillment, however, I was unsuccessful in rekindling his interest.

For any of you who continue to doubt the power of the lie, hark back a few years and recall the celebrated, sensuous, nonconformist actor with a penchant for dark, exotic flowers who picked one such specimen as his bride. You may remember that she claimed to have been born in some remote town in India, to be an orphan or not know the whereabouts of her parents, and several other touching biographical tidbits. However, as you may also remember, before long her plain, everyday mother and father surfaced with a far less exotic account of the circumstances, stripping the raven-haired beauty of her mystery and appeal.

If you have propensities in the direction of this primer and follow the above suggestions, you too can advance from a good to a great liar, with all the alienation and rejection possibilities it can offer.

Primer #9: Waiting for Prince Charming (The Greener Pastures Syndrome)

"There is always someone better than anyone you could possibly get."

—J.K.

Though I know of no comparative research studies, done under controlled laboratory conditions, to substantiate my point, it is my educated guess that, next to Primer #1, this one accounts for more rejection gratification than any other. In fact, if used according to instructions by practically anyone with a tendency to set unrealistic goals, it is difficult to see how it can fail.

The purpose of this attitude is to enable you to upgrade your inclination, to try to hit targets too high above you, to the point where it becomes a firm resolve, and hopefully an obsession. With definite guidelines to help you establish improbable targets for your individual cases, chances are 20 to 1 you won't hit them. In addition, since all other prospects will be met with indifference or disdain, you can see the enormous rejection possibilities inherent in this primer.

Selecting the Star Target

Practically any frank and friendly spinster can tell you how well the waiting-for-Prince-Charming approach works, but as in every rejection situation, individual criteria and penchants play a major role. One person's dross may be another's gold. Still, there are some generalities that may obtain for one and all, whatever your star target. In making your choice, try to choose someone:

1. From a category or situation in life that you rarely have occasion to encounter.

2. Whom you may encounter from time to time but in a position or situation so far removed that you only rate an occasional nod.

3. Whom you might see irregularly without ever being included in his life, social or otherwise.

4. Who you know is in a very elite and limited group, especially when the target is surrounded by an oversupply of determined women.

In general, train your sights on anyone you know in your heart there is hardly a chance in hell you can ever get.

Once you have chosen your star target, and made it known to the world at large, you must resolve firmly not to be deterred, realizing that there will be many forces working against you, trying to lessen your determination. Friends and relatives alike may point out that your goal is unrealistic. Unacceptable men you may sometimes date while waiting for Mr. Impossible could tempt you to give up your goal. People will hesitate to invite you, rightly feeling you wouldn't fit, given your splendid isolation.

However, although this is what you *really* want in your heart of hearts—that is, *not* to be invited, but to be pitied and rejected—conscious-level tendencies to relent and settle for less may be at work within you. In order to reinforce your resolve not to settle for less than the very best (remember the ad?), I suggest that you:

1. Downgrade and ridicule the men that less discriminating friends have chosen. Go on record as preferring ten times over to remain alone (remember Garbo!) than to get involved with some nondescript.

2. Be specific about the attributes you have in mind for

anyone you might choose, affirming that no lesser types need apply.

3. Decline all invitations to meet someone who does not meet your rigorous specifications.

4. If you meet someone you are attracted to, start fantasizing about how much better it would be with Prince Charming.

Fantasizing, in fact, is one of your most useful tools in the successful application of this primer. Take the case of Anna A., a woman in her thirties who *had* settled for less and was married to a nice, decent, but lusterless man, with whom she had two lovely children. But she was fed up with her routine life and began to imagine that she was having an affair with a famous young singer, whom she had actually never met. She purchased all his records and mooned around the house, listening to them instead of performing her dreary household chores. After a time, she began to tell her children that the singer was actually their father (which her seven-year-old broadcast throughout the neighborhood) and that they would soon be going away with him. In the final days, before she was taken to a quiet room without sharp objects, she had gone to his opening in a nearby city and disrupted it, threatening his wife, among other antics.

The point here, of course, is that it's never too late to apply the Prince Charming primer. If you failed to use it early in life, for whatever reason (probably because this book was not available in time to turn you on to it), don't despair: like Anna A., you can still apply it later on, especially if you are bent on destroying home and marriage. Take a careful look at the man you've been living with all these years, the man hidden behind the morning paper or slouched in front of the evening boob-tube: Does he really look (or act) like Prince Charming?

Get to work!

Generally speaking, in applying the Prince Charming primer, try to make sure your aim exceeds your possibilities—and that, of course, is something each of you will have to determine for yourself. The safest rule of thumb here is this: If your targets constantly ignore you, turn their backs when they see you coming, or at most give you the faintest of nods, your aim is okay. If you find your target responds or reciprocates, your aim is doubtless too low. In which case, move it up.

So much for the primers, or attitudes. But remember, they are only that. They are merely the first, basic steps toward nonfulfillment. There is still much to be learned, both theoretically and practically, specifically and generally, before you can venture forth into the world confident in the knowledge that you can, with almost computerlike efficiency, alienate anyone, at any time, in any situation.

Vertical Alienation

Most women wrongly assume that failure is easy and rejection simple, that anyone armed with a basic knowledge of general principles can arrive at successful nonfulfillment in virtually any situation. General principles do help, but as you advance down the thorny but rewarding path of alienating men, specific situations and areas require special skills. I have divided the areas of encounter with men into two broad categories: Vertical Alienation, embracing all those techniques that can be used in a standing or sitting position; and Horizontal Alienation, which is treated separately in Part III. I know that many of you may be eager to proceed to Part III directly, but there is much delicious pain and heartache to be found in the five areas covered here: the office, vacations, parties, automobiles, and tête-à-têtes.

The Office:
Behavioral Skills

I am assuming that you have selected with care the correct basic successful-failure attitude, or attitudes, from the alienation primers described in the previous section. Bring those contrary feelings and sour philosophies to the office every day. Given the amount of time you spend on the job, and the numbers of people you are thrown into contact with, the office is rife with possibilities for rejection fulfillment (RF).

Utmost office efficiency for maximum RF must be perfected on two behavioral levels. The first, General Objectionable Behavior, is geared to assure that you will make an unfavorable impression and establish a bad reputation among your fellow workers (of both sexes). The second, Specific Counterproductive Routines, details activities that directly involve the assumed target and will assure you the rebuff you seek.

General Objectionable Behavior

Research has shown that one of the things people most resent in their co-workers is selfish, inconsiderate, uncooperative behavior. Therefore, the more ways you can find to demonstrate these office skills, the better. Following are some suggestions:

• When there is an important rush project that has everyone swamped, develop a headache or other malady and leave early, preferably at noon.

• As often as possible, come in late and leave early (perhaps leaving your coat downstairs or in an outer room and pretending to "step out for just a moment" in the evening;

45

asking someone to turn on your light and muss your papers in the morning). However . . .

• Any time your colleagues ask *you* to cover for their extended lunch hour so they can run an errand, pretend you forgot and get them into trouble. Or tell them you'd rather not be involved.

• Regularly tie up the switchboard with personal calls, especially when someone is waiting for an important report from you. But whenever you receive a personal call for someone else, respond abruptly, and get all messages bollixed, unless they completely slip your mind. (Or take an inordinate interest in everyone else's calls: "Oh, is this Mrs. Smith's husband? . . . Oh, no?" Or ask prying questions.)

• Whenever you see people by the elevator with their coats on, ask if they are going out, and if so will they run an errand for you. If they hesitate, say, "Oh, never mind!" But whenever you leave the office, sneak out as inconspicuously as possible, before someone asks *you* for a favor.

• Always speak condescendingly about the job and say how you could never stay on such a job for very long—especially to the oldest employees there. Constantly rave about your house or apartment (bring in photos) or the posh hotel where you recently vacationed. Two or three times a week talk about quitting. Say, "Luckily, I don't have to work."

• Initiate air-conditioning arguments by always being unable to tolerate the temperature everyone else finds comfortable.

• Share with old-fashioned, pre-sex-revolution women colleagues the intimate details of your frequent weekend trips with an ever-changing cast of characters.

• Regularly fall madly in love, circulating photos, showing gifts, and singing the praises of one true love—until another one comes on the scene and the cycle starts again.

• Try to have an affair with all the new employees (after you have been through the old ones).

• When you really want to look your best, let no girdle or bra restrict your ample proportions. Be proud of your whistle-bait figure even if the response is only of peanut-gallery quality.

• Confide to female co-workers the number of executives who have taken you out (especially the married ones).

Specific Counterproductive Routines

When you have become proficient in the General Objectionable Behavior already detailed, study the following CPRs. Together, they will offer you complete, two-pronged protection from virtually any meaningful relationship that might otherwise evolve from office contacts and situations.

Having an Affair with the Boss

Because so many successful failures have observed the high rate of disaster arising from having affairs with the boss, this is one of the most popularly performed office routines not only in America but around the world.

If your boss is single and has a reputation for being serious, be sure to start the rejection-inviting behavior immediately after the onset of the affair. In general, to ensure the desired results, whenever you are alone together, burden him with unpleasant details about the office. Complain about co-workers who you feel have done you some injustice. Nag him to fire a girl you don't like for some vague reason. Try to wangle a raise from him. Ask him point blank about the rumors that he is about to lose a vital account. Attempt to learn details about important business secrets. (When the affair doesn't work out, reveal these to his competitors, thus ruining your name throughout the industry.) Give him extensive advice on a subject you have no background in. If he is married, nag him to take you to his country club, or to invite you to his house with a trumped-up escort for dinner, or to an intimate party he is giving. Pick at him about the status of his marriage and his *real* intentions with you. If you live at home and he is married, slyly arrange for your mother and father to be coming in as he picks you up in front of the house and pointedly introduce him to them. In addition, study the section of this book devoted to self-defeating behavior before, during, and after the sex scene: Horizontal Alienation.

Immediately after having started the affair with the boss, begin bossing everyone else around. Work irregular hours and stay out at the slightest provocation, often failing to inform fellow employees who will have to make up your work. Come in all gussied up as if you were going to a party, and do so little work it may seem you are already there. Or, conversely, overdo the hard-worker routine, assuming the duties of others, perhaps making it possible to lay off some of the staff, as if you personally shared in the profits. Make certain that any improper intramural conduct, scandal, or rumor around the office gets back to the boss forthwith. To ensure that your special status is not lost on any of the staff who do not seem sufficiently impressed, make suggestive remarks to the boss in their presence—even though he is obviously embarrassed by them—or take to staging lovers' quarrels within earshot of the others.

If all this fails and it becomes apparent that you do indeed have a special place in your boss's heart, begin pushing him to break up with his wife. When he points out that she has controlling stock in the company, knows too much about his tax manipulations, has threatened to take him to the cleaners in any divorce proceedings, or has gotten him to promise not to leave until the children—ages four and six—are grown up, decide to act positively. Write an anonymous poison-pen letter to his wife telling her all about you, to force his hand. Of course, you know that when it is forced, chances are a hundred to one you will receive the back of it. And in no time at all you will be experiencing the utmost in complete rejection fulfillment, for not only will you be out of a man, you will also be out of a job.

Traveling with a Petticoat Convoy

If for any reason you cannot consider having an affair with the boss, and if you tend to get along well with your co-workers, there is another counterproductive activity you can engage in with almost equally impressive results. It involves traveling around—during lunch hours and coffee breaks and even after office hours—with a convoy of "girls." Since there is safety in numbers, men who try to talk to you will be overwhelmed, and even intimidated, by the sheer force of woman power.

If no such petticoat convoy exists in your office setup, organize one. Given the large numbers of women who do not have regular dates (including some married women looking for more social activity), it should be easy for you to enlist a goodly assortment of women from your office to file around with you during and after the office day. Reserve a large table for lunch at a nearby restaurant once a week. And then there is the theater party, with each of your recruits bringing a girl friend if you want to swell your ranks.

Also, you can organize an office club for volley ball or other team sports, or a bridge club with the girls. Attend—en masse—dancing classes once a week at the "Y," or swimming or fencing classes. Or karate. (Yes, karate!)

While you are marching around with the brigade, tell yourself that you are only doing this to keep busy while waiting for the right man to come along. Actually, you know that even if he did he would probably not be able to get near you, given the sea of femininity forever surrounding you.

Even if all the girls are "fun loving," and their expressed intentions are to meet someone "nice," have an unspoken agreement on what to do if ever a hapless man manages to pierce the perimeter of the pack. Immediately divert all conversation to events that occurred on your previous outings, or other details with which he is totally unfamiliar. Concentrate on inside jokes, unsharable secrets, and whispered observations that evoke hunching activity and unexplained peals of laughter.

If the Brave New Arrival appears interested in you, assure the girls at bill-paying time that they needn't bother, your BNA will take care of it. Also, make it a firm policy to show your esprit de corps by not breaking flank and permitting a man to separate you from the pack.

Always manage to have two or three women pals hovering around your desk, discussing some phase of planning for this or that evening maneuver with les girls.

As further protection, select one of the least attractive members of your petticoat brigade, based on the probability that she will be less temperamental and competitive, and strike up a closer alliance. Hold long telephone conversations with her on strategy on how to get a man, so that any who may be trying to reach you can't get through. If anyone establishes communication and invites you out, burden him with the responsibility of finding a blind date for her, describing her as "beautiful," without bothering to explain that you refer to inner and not immediately visible qualities.

If any prospects from the office invite you out for lunch, bring her along, explaining that she doesn't go out much and is lonely. Before long you should notice that, out of a sense of understanding and compassion, he will make it obvious that he plans to let you spend more time with her—without him.

Counterproductive Character Roles

Certain counterproductive character roles have won such general negative acclaim in the offices in which they have been featured that you will doubtless want to study them for acting tips and guidelines. They can each be "replicated," * that is, re-created in their exact form; or aspects of each can be incorporated, as necessary, into these and other types of cross-character roles appropriate for all neurotic needs.

Peggy Pop-Up

Peggy Pop-Up would probably be surprised and indignant to see her character type high among those considered successful-failure models. For she firmly believes her carefully planned, meticulously executed, leave-nothing-to-chance method of acting to win men very effective. (What about the articles in *Cosmopolitan,* among other magazines, where the girls frankly admitted the scheming that was necessary to land their fabulous men?)

But what Peggy Pop-Up does not take into consideration—and what you also must ignore if you assume her role—is that if your intentions are so obvious that even the village idiot could not fail to detect them, even he would not fall.

With this in mind, the next time an interesting new executive (or anyone else who you know would normally never notice you) passes through your typing pool, decide then and there that he is for you. And remain undaunted by the fact that, though you manage to pass right by him, all smiles, five or six times over the next few days, he doesn't even acknowledge your existence. . . . Wait: Peggy Pop-Up thrives on adversity (attitude expertly pre-primed with the unrealistic-goals finish). The next time you see him going into the boss's office, casually station yourself outside the door perusing some presumably im-

---

* A term I first came upon during research on my subject in Vienna with Dr. Otto Partz, the famed Austrian psychologist whose experiments in character imitation, using chimpanzees and mandrills, are fascinating. I refer readers to his forthcoming book, *Primatenreplikation und Schimpansenachbildung.*

portant papers. When you hear him coming out, pretend to be looking for something on the floor—preferably from a semi-stooped position over which he might stumble. If you see him approaching while you are making coffee at the percolator, let out a high-pitched squeal as he passes by, as if you have burned yourself.

As soon as you find out who his secretary is, become chummy with her. Compliment her on her clothes, pick up her check for lunch, and stop by to see if she wants anything if you're going out—even though she's three floors above you and has worked there five years, and you have never before so much as nodded at her.

When you feel you are looking especially fetching, find an excuse to go sit at her desk and talk—keeping her from her work—hoping to get a glimpse of him. (Or, more important, hoping he will get a glimpse of you.) Don't be offended if, when he does, he tells his secretary not to have friends visiting during office hours. If that happens, simply keep in touch by phone.

If his secretary looks at you as though you're crazy when you suddenly begin trying to befriend her, think back to those late-night movies when Joan Crawford always got the boss in the end (even though he told her at first that her perfume, "Temptation," may be so considered in some quarters, but . . .). Remember how he later became mad for her—especially after she returned from Paris with the right perfume and a different accent—and they moved to the best house in the most snobbish section of town. Keep in mind, too, the old adage, "Nothing ventured, nothing gained." *

At five, lurk in the hall by the elevator he uses, waiting for him to come out (even though you may have no actual business on that floor). Once inside the car, try to accidentally brush against him (heaven *sur glace*) or step on his foot—even though the car is uncrowded. Make a big, and

* The misapplication of old adages can be honed to a fine art, as we shall see the further we progress in our successful-failure course.

hopefully unforgettable, fuss over how sorry you are.

Frequent the same restaurant he does for lunch, if possible at a table within earshot of his, and ask the waiter what he's having. When he tells you, order the same thing. Or go in with a fellow worker and engage in some conversation, possibly in an affected tone of voice calculated to impress him.

If you are not sure where he eats, solicit the help of one of the office gossips to stand out in front of the building until he comes out and follow him wherever he goes. When her mission succeeds, casually saunter over to the table next to him and act surprised to see him there.

Try to find out something about his current love interest, perhaps from someone you have seen him talking to but do not know very well. And try to learn what his financial status is—what kind of car he drives, the type of apartment he has, etc.

At some point in the above maneuvers, your target should begin to notice you—although frequently not in the way you may have planned. However, tell yourself you can always make up for any unfavorable impression he may have once you get to know each other better. With this thought in mind, continue to the next role.

Chatty Cathy

Now that you "more or less" know each other, it is time to get the relationship on a little more friendly basis. One way you might do this is to pretend you are unable to open the ladies' room door the next time you are there and spot him coming down the hall. Turn it the wrong way quickly as hard as you can, and hope it is a little jammed. Or pretend that you have misplaced your key and ask him if perhaps the men's room key might fit. Start a conversation about how you don't want to ask any of the girls you work with because they protect their keys as if they were gold, and perhaps extend this to the fascinating topic of how no one is willing to help anyone these days. Or complain about how difficult the girls on your floor are to work with, perhaps confiding to him that they are all jealous of you.

Once you have established this beachhead, try to strike up conversations with him whenever you see him. If you are able to extract any information from him about any of his interests—fishing, boating, gourmet cooking, pro football, or whatever—buy a book and bone up on it. Then, any time you are within five feet of him, try to slip something in on the subject. Say (or, preferably, shout), if football is the ploy, "What did you think of that down-and-out pattern Joe called in the third quarter?" Ask him pertinent questions, even on the crowded elevator, on this topic.

When you begin to notice that whenever he sees you waiting for the elevator he suddenly realizes he has left something back in his office—or when he tells you he has a toothache the next time you try to engage him in conversation, even on one of his favorite topics—come to the reluctant conclusion he must have "someone else." But instead of giving Norman from Accounting a break (he's been bugging you for two years to go out with him), zero in on another far-out prospect. Concentrate on how you can pop into his life for a series of rejections while more likely prospects are ignored.

Aggressive Anna

This character bears a superficial resemblance to Peggy Pop-Up, but the differences are legion: she seems at first glance more practical, her target selection being someone whom, by most standards, she could realistically hope to attract. He may even work in a nearby department, or seem accessible for other reasons. However, Anna is so Northwest-Mounted-Police aggressive she scares a man off instead of always getting her man. Play her accordingly.

The second time you see someone you think looks interesting, waste no time starting a conversation with him. Corner him by the water cooler and even if you do not yet know his name greet him with a warm "Hello there." By the fourth conversation, have him informed about all the things you like to do, what a great cook you are, what a terrific view you have from your terrace, and similar vital statistics, and press for the same data from him.

If he doesn't ask you out, get tickets to a show you know he'd love to see even if you have to pay scalpers' prices because reservations are sold out for months in advance. Or just happen to have two tickets to a star-studded museum opening, but your boy friend was called out of town suddenly . . . Or make him another offer he can't refuse . . .

. . . If he does, try to impress him with the people you know, people he could meet through you. For instance, work into the conversation that you were home all day Sunday trying to get your land legs back after having spent Saturday on a friend's boat (mention that his girl friend is an old school chum of yours so he won't think he's competition). Remark that you are surprised that you got seasick since the boat's so large and sleeps ten. (Make it large enough to be ocean-going, so that if he comes over you can begin the relationship with a lie that friend boat-owner has cruised off for some warmer clime.) Or mention the name of a famous person you visited recently, though you only met him in passing eight years prior.

Holly Hard-to-Get

If you see yourself as a species of living doll, a kind of American dream girl, office edition (even if your impressions are not generally shared), you may feel miscast in chaser roles like those already described and demand only chasee parts. In this case, you would be well advised to study the method-acting approach of Holly Hard-to-Get, sometimes known as Betty Busy. She presents herself as such a formidable challenge most men eventually decide it seems impossible and leave her alone . . . at last.

No matter how many superlative-filled rave notices you may rate or receive, if aspiring co-stars conclude it will take a federal case to get the role, most should decide just to forget the whole production.

Setting the stage for this characterization, the more frustrating barriers and seemingly insurmountable obstacles (rigid social rules, etc.) you can manage to construct between you and the hopeful leading man, the better. For example, you could have an established, inflexible position against letting men engage you in conversation (even in the relatively informal setting of the office) before being introduced; or ever giving your phone number out before several requests have been forthcoming. (Or, instead of giving your own number, give one where a message could be left, or ask for his; promise to call, but don't.)

If you are introduced to a prospect, especially if he looks interesting, remain somewhat aloof lest he think you are too anxious. Try to convey the idea that you are very aware that you have *le grand choix*—though you may have successfully alienated practically every decent prospect on the scene.

When someone you have met stops to talk, encourage any other men around, whom you know also like you, to join you, to show how popular you are. If there is no one around to play supporting roles, maneuver the conversation around to talk about your fabulous night before— a fantastic theater premiere, a party of famous celebrities, dinner at an exclusive membership club, etc. (Clearly you are not the type to settle for a hamburger in the Village.)

Any time you relent and accept an invitation for lunch— see "The Last Supper (Out)" for guidelines—try to include in the conversation, centered mainly around your busy social life, at least one tale on some chap who is chasing you though you are not really interested in him. Explain, however, that you don't know quite how to tell him. Or tell a "little devil" story about yourself, about how you played a naughty trick on some unsuspecting man without his realizing it.

If you decide to give someone your telephone number, always include an assortment of rules and regulations with it: do not call before nine p.m.; call only between six and seven p.m. on Tuesdays and Thursdays; or call only on the weekends, but never before twelve on Saturdays, etc. And never on Sunday.

Whenever anyone calls for a date, recite your busy schedule to show it will be something of a chore to fit the caller in. Wind up putting him on standby, telling him you will let him know. When you have finally decided to go out with him, play twenty questions when he arrives: Where is the party? Who will be there? How well does he know the host? Or what has he planned for the evening? Does he have reservations anywhere? Is anyone else coming along? If so, who are they and what do they do?

In the event there is a bar or club where you are well known, always take your date there for a nightcap so you can show off and be the center of attention. Leave him, to table hop among the ol' gang of yours. Or worse still, invite various friends to join you for drinks—on him.

On the way home begin talking about how exhausted you are because this is the third time this week that you have been out. If you can't wait a few dates more for rejection fulfillment, stifle a yawn, but barely.

Of course you are too "pooped" to invite him in even for a moment. Besides, by now the evening is on the downgrade, having peaked when you were "on" with your friends earlier.

Even if you have a face that could launch a thousand battleships and a body that could turn them around, a bit part of this role should get you X'd-out ratings with fellow office workers, lawyers, and Indian chiefs alike.

Through it all, your friends will be saying what a beautiful, fun-loving girl you are and wondering why you can never keep a man. Never will they know that all the while you have planned it that way!

Evelyn Ever-Young

No list of office types would be complete without Evelyn Ever-Young. She is the one who counts only every other birthday, thinks makeup was invented to mask the aging process, and dresses accordingly. She has lying about her age down to such a science that she invariably remembers to feign ignorance of any movie, song, or recorded historical event before the 1950s. She claims to have come to New York only sixteen years ago—right out of college.

Her age? It seems a little gremlin snuck into the personnel files and scratched it out. Though she claims to be thirty-eight, it was remarked by one of the office statisticians that Evelyn once let it slip that she had worked on her last job on Wall Street for twenty-two years; since she had worked in her present job for fourteen, her career would have to have started when she was two.

However, that these Evelyns are young at heart, and prefer all things young, including men, few can deny. Many women, not wanting to face advancing age, feel they can fend off Father Time more effectively with the energetic assistance of a strong young man. Since the office is an excellent place to recruit young blood (pretending to take them under your wing, with other parts of the anatomy to follow), if you are of the age and inclination, the Evelyn Ever-Young role might well be for you.

By observing the *modus operandi* of one Evelyn E. with whom I once worked, you should be able to get a number of ploys and pointers that could serve you in good stead.

I ran into Evelyn not long ago. I had not seen her for some time, and with advancing years she was letting her hair grow until the curls, held with a red, white, and blue ribbon, now bounced midway down her back. Her navy blue mini-dress featured white collar and cuffs, and with white boots she was ready to board the parochial-school bus. Of course, since practically everyone loves to dress young in these times—I refuse to give up knee socks and short pants myself—her attire would not have been so important had I not seen, after we began to chat, that she was up to her old tricks with young men. For, though I carefully avoided the subject, she did manage to mention a young man she had helped through college, who had fled to Europe immediately upon receiving his degree. That was two years ago. Before that, there had been the marvelous young but "level-headed" one who wanted her to become his partner in the accounting firm he was setting up—for which she co-signed his loan. He turned out to be very married, a fact she discovered too late, when she went to his house. She did not mind finding he had a wife, she said; it was seeing the two children, dog, cat, and pet guinea pig that got her, and she promptly decided that he, at age thirty-one, was too settled for her anyway.

At the time of our meeting she was combing the neighborhood for an empty apartment for a (needless to say) young man recently transferred to the home office from an out-of-town subsidiary. She thought it would be nice to surprise him with news of an apartment, since he had been having such trouble finding one himself. Meanwhile, under her arm she carried a report she planned to type for him over the weekend (to keep her busy lest she meet some more mature man who might adore her *joie de vivre* and Ever-Young spirit).

The next time we met, a few months later in a department store, she was on the muscular arm of a tall, very attractive man. As she spoke with me in her usual effervescent manner, her friend, after acknowledging our introduction, wandered off to the kid glove department. There was just time enough to ask if this was the "find" from the Midwest that she had spoken about at our last meeting. Oh no, she explained softly, *that* one had been *too* immature and had taken up with a little high-school dropout shortly after she, Evelyn, had managed to find him an apartment.

By now, fresh-face was drifting back, and soon they were lost in the crowd. While I do not know if the rumors that she is actually going on fifty are true, if they are—what a way to go! And what better evidence that achieving rejection fulfillment does not have to be all work and no play.

Meddlesome Mattie

For this role it is necessary that you accumulate as much knowledge as you can about as many of your fellow workers as possible. And, while even minor details and tidbits should not be ignored, the more intimate your facts, the better.

When you are with a co-worker prospect, share the juicy gossip you have garnered. Confide in him who is sleeping with whom, who used to sleep with whom, and who would like to sleep with whom (for each of the above categories, explain why). Try to include at least three or four deep secrets that you were honor bound not to reveal.

Be the self-appointed statistician on how long girls (or men) you work with have been married before their first child arrives. Don't neglect rumors pertaining to their family either. To keep the record straight, simply preface such offerings with "You know what I heard?" in a low and secretive voice.

To avoid the possibility of anyone's thinking you are malicious, say what a shame a particular piece of information is, possibly softening the impact with "and she is such a lovely person."

After having confided all the latest about everyone else in the office, zero in on your target's personal and private life with a series of intimate and prying questions—which from your previous revelations he knows will become tomorrow's exposés.

Your Meddlesome Mattie performance should prove especially gratifying from two points of view. First, if you are able to cast aspersions on everyone else, you will be able to feel superior by comparison. Second, you know, at least subconsciously, that unless your target is considering opening a newspaper with a gossip column, it is unlikely he'll want to be associated with someone so obsessed with other people's personal business. Therefore, you can count, as surely as night follows day, on his ultimate rejection.

Clara Career

Since commitment to a career need not necessarily interfere with your social life or marriage opportunities, to assure rejection you must play the role as if your heart were a time clock, your brain a computer, your soul the alter-soul of your boss, and your body the corporate body, with copy-machine fluid flowing in your veins. Here's how:

1. Gauge your success as a person on how well you succeed in your career, and let your entire life revolve around it.

2. Any time you go out with a target, bring your business troubles with you. Or, if the situation is bright, paint and repaint this picture all evening. Even if your career is glamour and you are its epitome, your target will soon become weary of details about your "fantastic" session with the photographer doing the cover story, your latest interviews, contracts you are torn between, etc.

3. Take your career home with you, even (or especially) if you live alone. If ever someone calls for a date, consider it a career interference.

4. Though always threatening to buy dressier clothes, invariably wind up with something more suitable for the office.

5. If you are in a career dominated by men—as most careers are—counteract the suspicion that you may be motivated by a desire to get a man by defeminizing yourself

as much as possible. Select clothes that neutralize your best curves; switch to matronly, reserved hair styles; see your local optometrist in the hope you may need glasses (the heavier the rims, the better).

The
Vacation Threat

There is no limit to the potentially dangerous consequences of an improperly planned vacation. The case history of Helen R. demonstrates this point all too well.

A somewhat plain but not unattractive teacher in a private school, Helen was well-read, an interesting conversationalist, a gourmet cook, and the proud possessor of a tastefully decorated apartment. However, at age thirty-three (often toned down to twenty-nine), she had managed to avoid any long-lasting romantic attachments. Then, after some years of urging by her college roommate (married), she unwisely decided to accept her invitation to spend a week's vacation in the small Nevada town in which her friend resided. (As if she had not been forewarned that eligible men outnumbered eligible women, doubtless accounting for her earlier reluctance to go.)

Not only did she now decide to accept, but in a moment of weakness she even made an appointment at one of those "A New You in 24 Hours"–type beauty shops. And while it cannot be said that she emerged a beautiful fairy princess, she did reappear considerably improved, with a more flattering hair style and greater self-confidence.

Helen arrived in Nevada in true "There's-a-New-Girl-in-Town" style, and was given a party, in which she played a role that was new for her: Belle of the Ball. Before the evening was over, and during the remainder of her two-week stay, she settled on a very eligible builder-friend of her hostess. Everything jelled so perfectly that she departed with heavy heart. Her chagrin was lightened, however, by her new friend's promise to extend a forthcoming Washington business trip to include New York.

Several letters later, he arrived.

Fortunately, however, just when things looked ominous (that is, bright) Helen saved the day; once back on home turf, she reverted to her neurotic, alienating ways, forgot the beauty shop, and let her self-confidence wilt. At last report, she had turned the relationship around and escaped by the skin of her teeth.

The moral of this story and the warning it conveys is this: avoid vacation sites where there may be eligible men, unless you know they are outnumbered by desperate women at least three to one.

In this enlightened spirit, when planning your next vacation, consider one of those irresistibly advertised "Singles Playgrounds." "TURN YOUR VACATION INTO A HAPPENING," one suggests provocatively. Or "ESCAPE TO THE SUN, LOVE, AND FUN." Another may inquire rhetorically, "WOULD YOU LIKE NEW FRIENDS, A NEW LIFE, GOOD FOOD, AND GREAT ENTERTAINMENT?" Or, more to the point, "BORED?"

What such advertisements fail to reveal, of course, is that most of your newfound friends are apt to be either women looking for the same thing you consciously claim to be, or an odd assortment of male losers and escaped husbands in disguise. (You will sometimes be able to recognize one of the latter by the lighter circle around the third finger of his left hand; but you can, if you like, always fall for the story that he is recently divorced.) In the unlikely event you do meet someone suitable, you have the subsequent chapters of this book to guide you in effectively ruining any burgeoning relationship.

Another suggested vacation plan might center around an extended excursion with a group of people with whom you have little or nothing in common. Try to figure out what you dislike most in the world, then hook up with a charter group catering to just that. If the notion of climbing into a dinghy makes you queasy, consider joining an ocean-going sailboat for a week of fun and games. If you have notably weak ankles, join a ski charter to Switzerland for a week or two. If your dainty skin blisters at the slightest exposure to the sun, head for the Caribbean with only a bikini as luggage. All this, of course, won't guarantee a ruined vacation (there's always the chance that the doctor in the hospital to which you've been rushed . . .), but each little step counts. Go preferably in midsummer, on the theory that not only is it cheaper but, if you do happen to meet someone there, you will have no competition. Naturally, all the while you are making plans, you really know that no moderately solvent man in his right mind is likely to consider such a trip, particularly if he is in the market for a new girl. You can therefore be confident you will be able to spend your time sweltering in your island paradise alone and unthreatened.

Consider, too, the possibility of spending your vacation at your elderly aunt's lodge. Convince yourself it is a clever idea because with the money you save you can stay twice as long, and ignore the probability that the extra time will only add up to more days of boredom, since you will have to spend the majority of your time with Auntie. Besides, since she is almost surely from the old school, even if you do somehow manage to unearth some target, you will have to contend with raised eyebrows and embarrassing questions if your conduct does not conform to her rigorous standards.

Or reject all these plans and spend your winter scouting around for one of the sub-low-priced vacation tours that offer Europe on pennies. You may have to take a vow of poverty to qualify, but don't let that deter you. On this one you can relax in the knowledge that even if you should meet anyone, he will doubtless be so poverty-stricken he'll be solely occupied with trying to make ends meet. (This one is especially recommended if your announced goal is to meet and marry a millionaire.)

As you can see, only by careful planning can you be certain to counteract the threat that a delightful vacation could constitute.

Remember, a carefully planned vacation is a safe vacation!

The Party Scene

Nothing affords greater feelings of accomplishment than leaving a party alone, after successfully alienating everyone who came near you. In my opinion, this is as near the ultimate in complete rejection realization as you are ever likely to get.

However, many of you may understandably prefer the more drawn-out sensations of rejection over a longer period of time, and prefer simply to set the forces of rejection in motion at the first party meeting.

Beneath the frivolous, deceptively harmless surface of the party scene lurk many threats to a girl's resolve not to become "meaningfully" involved with a man. Yet, for those who are properly trained and equipped, the party scene offers unique opportunities to ruin potential, and even thriving, relationships. If you wish to derive the most from such festive occasions, study this section diligently. Only after you have will you find that a party can really be a ball.

Party Pitfalls

In view of the number of opportunities for experiencing rejection at most parties, if you play your cards right you can often receive sufficient rejection gratification to last you for weeks. But, as in most situations, you must have expertly designed primary and contingency plans to avoid specific pitfalls. (Male chauvinist though he was, Napoleon had a point when he admonished his marshals, "Not just primary battle plans, Messieurs, but contingency plans to fall back on in case of dire need!")

In accordance with your special neurotic requirements, you should always establish a clear order of priorities. In going to parties—and by "parties" I mean any social occasion, be it a dinner, cocktails, swinging singles, etc.— you must realize that by their very nature your exposure to a large number of presumably eligible men is a foregone conclusion. Thus you can never relax your guard.

Alienate the Hostess

One of the best ways to deal with the party-pitfall problem is to alienate the host (or hostess) with all due speed. For if you inadvertently make a good initial impression, you will increase the likelihood of his (or her) introducing you to the most promising targets present. But if you are sufficiently shrewd to alienate him (or her) at every turn, not only will he (or she) not introduce you to anyone, she (or he) may actually warn off any interested party by telling him how objectionable you are.

If, for example, you have a coat that your hostess offers to take, follow her to the place she intends to deposit it and ask for a safer place. Suggest she find a hiding place for your purse (which you should clutch to your bosom as though holding Fort Knox). If the other coats are on a bed or crowded into a closet, insist that she find some place where yours will not be crushed.

This should certainly dampen any enthusiasm she may have had about introducing you to any eligible men, but to drown it completely, appoint yourself a committee of one to appraise and criticize the festivities. Every time the hostess passes, particularly when she is loaded down with trays or otherwise occupied, stop her and share with her the benefit of your pregnant observations. Suggested topics to criticize: the music (too fast, or too slow and draggy); the number of guests (too many, or too few). Ask, "Are any more people coming?" Evaluate the conduct of the guests and general conditions: "No one knows anyone else." "No one's dancing." "Couldn't you try to liven things up?" Or, alternatively: "The crowd is really getting rowdy. I'm not used to socializing with such people. Where *did* you find such odd types?" Inquire about things you do not see: food, your favorite Scotch, or a certain record album, as if she had some contractual obligation to furnish them for you.

Take it upon yourself to overrule any decision she may make regarding whether she wants the heat up (or down), or a certain lamp on (or off). Follow close behind her, changing things to your liking. If she closes the windows or doors, expressing concern about the possibility of disturbing the neighbors, open them when the merriment reaches a peak.

If you know you are inclined to be clumsy, take special interest in the more delicate articles and artifacts, handling and inspecting them endlessly, thus increasing the risk of breaking something valuable. Head for the overstuffed chair—the one without the slip cover—and there balance a plate of food on your knee while holding your drink precariously. Display a marked disregard for the dangers of cigarettes and cigarette ashes. Keep resting your burning cigarettes on the edge of some piece of (valuable) furniture, making sure your host sees you. Play the "How-long-an-ash can-I-make"? game, never flicking the ashes until the last minute . . . then onto the Persian rug.

If you want to be equally objectionable but more subtle, follow the hostess about, engaging her in friendly conversation and trying to monopolize her time as though you were her sole guest.

Graciously offer to invite some more interesting people to the host's next party. If you utilize any two or three of the above strategies, however, you will not have the problem of being asked to the next one yourself.

Forget Names

To make the right first impression, forget all names forthwith.*

Since psychiatrists have long taught that you do not forget the names of people who impress you favorably, most men will assume you are not interested in them if you continually call them by names other than their own, mispronounce their names, or use that old favorite, "What did you say your name was again?" Another offensive little game is that of confusing names and data of some alienation target, focusing on important or basic facts, to show you were not listening. For example, after telling a third party that Bob (whose name is Bill) went to Yale (when it was really Harvard), top it off with, "Bob here's a salesman for Ford" (when he's really an engineer for Chrysler).

When it becomes obvious to a man that his name simply cannot be registered on your brain, he will no doubt suddenly remember something he has to do. However, if for some unforeseeable reason he does stick around, assuming things can only get better, he might offer to get you a drink, either hoping to make a better impression on you or perhaps just wanting to get away for a moment to reestablish his identity, at least to himself.

Even if he was undaunted by your failure to remember his name, he is certain to frown on your disappearing the moment he goes for your drink. If you can arrange it, let him find you in another room, cozily engaged in conversation with another target. If you are unable to find anyone with whom to strike up a conversation by the time he returns, retreat to the powder room to freshen up. Or go out on the terrace to admire the view, or do anything you can

---

* Here is a rule of thumb to help you forget names quickly: Immediately after meeting someone, decide that he does not look like his name and rename him mentally; or, remembering someone he reminds you of, assign him that name. It's simple, and it works like magic.

think of to leave him holding the bag—that is, the drink.

When and if he finally finds you, take a sip of the drink, then lodge an immediate complaint. Say, "Did they run out of Scotch?" Or, "What happened to the soda?" Or, "Who in the world mixed this drink?" (especially if you suspect he did). Always decline his offer to take it back and make any necessary changes, thus making it obvious that you are the type who prefers to complain about the one you have.

The Short-Answer Conversation Deterrent

No defense perimeter between you and any man you may meet at a party can be considered fully effective until you have learned how to employ SACD, the Short-Answer Conversation Deterrent. This is the strategy whereby the interested man's effort to develop a conversation is frustrated by your ability to make only brief, uninformative statements, without sufficient substance on which he might build a conversational assault. Even when he asks direct questions on subjects you might well be interested in (thus hoping to effect some relaxation of your defense), your response should always be minimal—whenever feasible only "Yes" or "No" (or, better yet, unintelligible grunts).

Some people seem to have been born with the dry, noncommittal character that makes them naturally proficient in this technique. Others, being plain dumb, use monosyllabic words for lack of ability to employ any others. If, however, you do not fall into either of these categories, following are some examples that should assist you in the development of your own short-answer technique.

Friend Betty comes up to introduce you to an attractive target whom she identifies as the friend she has spoken to you about, the one in insurance, as you were a few years ago. "You two should have a lot in common," she says, smiling, and departs.

If this conversation were allowed to travel its natural reckless pace between two people with something in common, amenities could quickly build up to such threatening proportions that before long he might be asking to take you home, or for a date, or at least for your phone number. But thanks to SACD:

HE (*smiling*): Well, I've heard so much about you I'd begun to think it was a conspiracy to create a legend.

YOU (*with a Mona-Lisa smile*): Oh?

HE: Yes, but I'm glad to be proven wrong tonight.

YOU: (*Silence*).

HE (*already slightly unsettled*): So, I'm told you worked for Sloan McPherson.

YOU: Um.

HE: How'd you like working for them?

YOU: Uh. Okay.

HE: Yes, yes. It's a good company, as my competitors go. . . . (*Here he will probably pause—a silence for you to ask what company he is with. Obviously, any interest expressed in his firm could develop into an hour-long conversation; thus you say nothing. He continues*): I'm with Baine Thompson.

YOU: Oh. (*This with a final, subject-is-closed ring.*)

HE (*remembering the books that counsel the would-be successful conversationalist to talk about things the other person has done*): How long were you with McPherson?

YOU: Two years.

HE: Two years, eh?

YOU: (*Silence*).

HE: Uh . . . what department were you in?

YOU: I was in research.

HE (*animated by this delayed demonstration that you are capable of formulating entire sentences*): Oh! Research! I'm in charge of sales, but I always thought the research end must be very fascinating.

YOU: It is.

HE: Well, well . . . what company are you with now?

YOU: Johns, Mitchell.

HE: Oh, I see. (*Then, repeating, "I see," to stretch the little he has to say as far as possible*): Are you still involved in research?

YOU: More or less.

HE: Well, you look like someone who would be great at figures. (*He laughs.*)

YOU: (*Unsmiling silence—any display of a sense of humor is out in this approach*).

HE: I knew a fellow who worked for Johns, Mitchell a few years back. . . . How long have you been with them?

YOU: Six months.

HE: Uh-huh. Well (*clearly sinking*), he would have been before your time.

YOU: Probably.

A dead silence will usually follow, as dead as any interest he may now have in you.

Or you are sitting on your tuffet, minding your curds and whey, when along comes this spider. Although you have never seen him before, he has such a familiar air it would be difficult to ignore him completely—he just might be an old acquaintance. So Short-Answer Conversation Deterrent to the rescue:

HE: Hi there. How are you?

YOU: Fine.

HE (*preferring to preserve the old-acquaintance aura*): Do you mind if I join you?

YOU: Not really.

HE: My name's Bob. (*Naturally, it's all on a first-name basis.*)

YOU (*politely*): Nice to meet you.

HE: I'm sure it would be nice to meet you, too.

YOU (*never seeing the other side of the double entendre*): Pardon me?

HE: I mean . . . it would be nice to know *your* name.

YOU: Oh, Mary.

HE: Well . . . what do you do, Mary, besides look beautiful? (*There is clearly a dearth of original material.*)

YOU: Secretary.

HE: What's the lucky company?

YOU (*whenever he begins to try to make an advance through flattery, meet his aggression with obvious detachment and disinterest. Look vacantly off into space, or as though searching for someone else. Then, considerably after he has paid you the compliment, ask*): What were you saying?

You will generally find that a little SACD goes a long way, and within minutes "he" will be off regaling someone else with his charms. (N.B. If, however, "he" persists, be forewarned there are some targets who live to talk and will love your short answers since it will afford them an opportunity to pour out a current of uninterrupted conversation. In such cases you may have to reverse your strategy and fall back on the rapid-fire nonstop-talker attack. See "The Verbal Overkill Technique.")

The D&Ls (Desperadoes and Lonelies)

There is a good possibility you may meet someone from this fringe group at a party. They are the crass bores, friendly failures, and other unaesthetic individuals who in their understandable loneliness are drawn toward party lights and promised companionship like moths to flame, notwithstanding the fact that frequently they get burned. In most cases, they were not actually invited to the party but found out about it through a telephone campaign in which they whiningly inquire to friend and foe alike, "You know about any parties tonight?"

If you meet such a person at a party, the usual alienation techniques—short answers, veiled insults, vacant looks—

may well fail, since he has accepted such subtle rejection strategies as a way of life.

Besides, your policy position vis-à-vis creeps should be not to alienate but indeed to attract them. As we shall see later, under "Clutterers," the more fugitives from the Most Unwanted List you can gather around you, the easier it will be for you to forfend any desirable candidates. Therefore, be at a loss for an excuse why you can't give Mr. Sadsack your phone number and, after stuttering and stammering a bit for form's sake (should anyone overhear), disclose it to him, thus accumulating one more clutterer in your life.

Partying with Your BF

Considering the possible dire consequences of improperly managed party encounters, you may prefer to attend them with a boy friend you have somehow not yet managed to alienate. Not only is he a buffer zone to anyone new; you can also seize the opportunity to alienate *him* by the display of repellent qualities he may not yet have observed.

When you take your BF to a party, you must be constantly on the alert to make sure that he doesn't have a good time with you, which would add a plus to his mental tally on you. Obviously, the course of the evening cannot be left to chance. It should be mapped out in consideration of various factors, including the seriousness of your relationship with your escort, the extent of his regard for the host's opinion of him, and perhaps most important, his personality.

You have two alternative ways to spoil things. If your BF is the outgoing, life-of-the-party type, you can clinging-vine it, hanging onto his arm and demanding his undivided attention all evening long. Or, after the first few dances, you can exhibit the self-sacrificing quality of your character by suggesting that he may want to mingle, and send him off on his own; with his charm, he's bound to find someone to replace you.

If, on the other hand, you know your escort mixes with people like oil with water, deposit him, shortly after arriving, in some lonely corner, to study the paintings on the wall or contemplate his hands in folded and unfolded positions. If at length he works up the courage to join you in some perky group, remember never to introduce him to anyone.

Parties also give you a wonderful opportunity to demonstrate your "way-with-people" technique. This involves casually strolling around with him until you come upon a fairly good-sized group engaged in pleasant conversation. You join them, pretending to be interested in the topic under discussion, but at the first opportunity you introduce the most controversial subject you can imagine.

Always be sure your position is the one with which the majority of those present would most vigorously disagree and, it is hoped, be offended by, but do not permit anyone to shake it. As the controversy heats, the voices may rise, alerting the host or hostess to potential danger. If he or she tries to intervene and perhaps minimize the differences, or suggests that everyone dance, remain firmly at your post, refusing to be swayed—or danced.

Often these acid discussions have a way of spilling over into other groups and eventually infesting the entire festivities. If this happens, you will usually notice the guests soon excusing themselves and heading for the room where the coats are kept. At this point, turn to your BF and elaborate further on your thinking, though his only response will probably be an icy glare.*

One technique I find especially suitable when you are with someone who has proposed (or seriously discussed) marriage with you is called the OFF (Openly Flirting with Friends) technique, the goal of which is to suggest to him

---

* This technique is especially recommended when the host or hostess is a close friend of your escort.

how you might amuse yourself while he is slaving away at the office.

Whenever your BF's friends are around, pick out one of the nicer ones and direct all your conversation to him, as you "tense" him with your direct stare and pretend to melt under his. Should ol' BF have the lack of grace to interject one of his own views, pretend to be so absorbed in your private tête-à-tête with his friend that you don't even hear him. Compliment his friend on his clothes, on his personality, and especially on his physique. Invite him to dance with you and study his eyes appreciatively as you float in his arms. Before he leaves, or you are escorted away, give him your phone number under the transparent pretense of wanting to introduce him to a girl friend.

If your escort has no interesting friend, strike up a friendship on your own, then dance repeatedly with this new target. Or do a disappearing act, where you wind up on the terrace or porch, or off on a get-acquainted stroll, from which you return with your hair slightly mussed, perhaps with his jacket thrown over your shoulders—or maybe even his arm, in which case make *sure* BF sees you coming back.

Also important: there is no place like a party, when everyone else is drinking and having a good time, to let your hair down and join the drinking. After you have had enough (what "he" may describe as too much), you will find that many party tricks, such as kissing all the cute fellas or doing your own interpretation of an Egyptian belly dance or Broadway striptease, come easy.

When your boy friend (the killjoy!) gets your coat and suggests it's time to leave, say, "Aw, c'mon, it's still early," and go off in search of another drink.

Finally, make it a general policy never to leave a party unless it appears certain that your BF is having a wonderful time and would love to stay forever. In which case: migraine time!

Rules of the Road, or How to Drive Him Crazy

No course in alienating men could be considered complete without some basic instructions in CCC: Correct Car Conduct, or Rules of the Road.

Realistically speaking, when you first get into a car with someone you will have to appear relaxed and friendly and show confidence in your driver. However, with a little imagination you can subtly set the wheels of an unpleasant mood in motion from the very beginning.

If he has opened the door for you, male-chauvinist style, get into the car but instead of unlocking his side, readjust the rear-view mirror to take a final makeup review. Then carefully place your pocketbook or any package you might have on the dashboard or the edge of the seat, where it can tumble down and distract him should he have to stop short.

Conversation

Select appropriate subjects to discuss as he drives. Recommended: any subject that would distract his attention; remarks about incidents, people, or buildings that he would have to look away from the road to see. Or (after having observed that he is the sensitive type) any topic that could prove unsettling, dwelling on serious accidents you have seen or read about, including at least one where the driver was the innocent victim. Or quote the appalling statistics on the increasing number of highway deaths, murderous alcoholics driving cars, etc. Finally, always try to find out how many wrecks *he* has had. (If he has never had any, he may start thinking of the "speak-of-the-devil-and-he's-bound-to-appear" theory; or, if he has had some, you will unpleasantly refresh his memory.)

All Clutched Up

A constant case of nerves will help you with this one.

Soon after getting into the car, appoint yourself co-driver in charge of speed control and all road conditions. Tell him how many miles an hour he is going. Read the signs along the highway that indicate correct speed. Keep him posted on all road dangers, real and imagined. ("The road is slippery; be careful when you put on the brakes or we may slide into that car in front." Or, "Let's not get too close to the shoulder because it looks soft.)

If he is driving at anything above a snail's pace, remind him of the radar on the roads. If it's a hot day, ask him about the possibility that the tires might overheat and blow out.

Call attention to objects along the road, as if you believed he would run over everything if you did not restrain him: "Look out, there's a woman." "Watch it, that car is about to pull out," or, "Oh, there's a dog over there."

Giving (and Keeping) Directions

Whenever you are directing him to a destination, never entrust him with all the information at once. Wait until he has almost passed the street where you are to turn and squeal, "Turn here! Turn here!" (Left turns described as right are, of course, highly recommended at such times; but if you forget, simply say, "Turn!" Omitting the specific direction is a sure-fire alienation technique.)

If you're not sure how to get where you are going, use your intuition in making the decisions. When it becomes clear that you are hopelessly lost, become resentful; if he suggests stopping to ask someone for more reliable directions, say, "What's the matter? Don't you *trust* me?"

If he asks your help in trying to get through a tight spot, *always* encourage him by telling him he can make it. If he misses and bangs or scratches the car, exonerate yourself by reminding him, "You're the one who's driving." Imply that a good driver could have made it.

If ever you are with a driver when he is involved in an accident, get out of the car and admit in front of everyone that it was your friend's fault. Remember to get the name of his insurance company, after confiding to him that you are not really injured. (You'll collect another cherished demerit by asking him to recommend a good attorney.)

If his driving is not, in your opinion, up to snuff and he has difficulty getting out of a tight spot, starting his car on an icy surface, trying to get into a tiny parking space, or whatever, say, "Shall I do it for you?"

If he plans to take you to visit friends who live some distance away, wait until the last minute to get dressed. (See "How to Play the Late Game.") When finally you get on the road, keep reminding him how late you are; suggest he cut in and out of traffic to make better time. Or ask, "Why are you poking along so?" when actually he is exceeding the speed limit.

Encourage him to "make" changing lights and turn where it's not permitted. If he is stopped by a policeman, don't hang back: get out and show how helpful you can be. Explain to the officer what actually happened. Say, "Officer, I was watching the speedometer and we were *not* exceeding the speed limit." If the officer does not agree, say, "Officer, when's the last time you checked *your* speedometer?" Remind him that he is a servant of the public and that you contribute to his salary. Take his badge number, name, and rank.

If your driver tries to be conciliatory or to make signs behind the policeman's back for you to be quiet, bring up past and present police scandals. Say, "Have you read *Serpico?*" Or, "I see where the ex-head of the vice squad got ten years for graft." Advise your date of his constitutional rights. After he gets his ticket, talk about it for the remainder of the evening, blaming him for not having been sufficiently firm.

New-Car Etiquette

Since a man's new car is sure to have a special place in his affection, there are certain techniques that are virtually guaranteed to make you lose *your* place in his affections.

1. Badger him to teach you to drive his car.

2. Create the right mood for the ride he is taking you on in his recently purchased, deluxe model, super-eight 400-HP job by gazing enviously out the window at perky small sports models zipping past. Say, "How much did you say you paid for this monster?"Or, "How many miles does this thing get to a gallon?" *

3. If, on the contrary, your date has a sports car, pretend not to know how to sit comfortably in it, what to do with your legs, or how to get in and out of it. Talk wistfully about a friend with a luxurious automobile and how spacious it is, as you move your head gingerly for fear of hitting his low roof.

4. At roadside snack stands, order overladen hamburgers-with-everything, or ice-cream cones (preferably "soft" ice cream), buttery popcorn, caramely candy, or

---

* Studies have shown how intimately and deeply men relate to their cars—thus are especially vulnerable in this area. Any deprecating references to their new babies—"thing," "tub," "rattletrap" are a few—will prove effective.

other gooey goodies to go, all of which will increase the likelihood of your leaving food "droppings" or sweet fingerprints around to remind him of you endearingly the next day.

5. Conduct an independent study of the dashboard, fiddling with gadgets and turning knobs to see what happens.

6. When the ride is over, ask him to let you borrow the car. Don't be surprised when he refuses; by now he is probably convinced that the place you should go to could not be reached by car.

FOWM*
as an
Art Form

At times, notwithstanding some women's complete dedication to failure, unabated longing for rejection fulfillment, and the best-laid counterproductive plans and attitudes as recommended herein, something goes awry. Then without warning a positive and unfulfilling relationship develops to threaten the lonely misery desired.

This could result from a number of things: a simple lack of vigilance or *sang froid;* failure to follow my instructions to the letter; a basic sensitivity in many women that instinctively rejects certain negative attitudes or behavior traditionally considered "wrong."

For you who fall into these categories, this chapter on the art of ferreting out (and becoming inextricably involved with) the wrong man is offered. Once the FOWM. technique has been mastered—even if this group chooses or inadvertently does everything right by the standards of Emily Post, or as embodied in the *Cosmopolitan* girl,— there is little likelihood that anything positive will result. This FOWM approach is also effective as a backup guarantee when used in conjuction with the other recommended methods.

The Married Man

If there were an international hall of fame to commemorate and epitomize wrong-man types for single women, the married man would rate a place of high honor. My respect

* Ferreting Out the Wrong Man

for their negative worth is so widely shared in successful-failure circles that married men are constantly being recruited and concentrated on as love objects by those pursuing the ultimate in suffering.

Some among you may already be enjoying a constant turnover of satisfyingly sorry relationships with a series of married men. However, I contend that superior gratification can be realized in the long-term, all-eggs-in-one-basket relationship involving one married man.

The following case histories should give you an idea of the possibilities in this area. In rating married men, I suggest classifying them from "A" to "E" according to the rejection possibilities they seem to offer—"A," of course, being those most inaccessible and fraught with problems.

As you peruse the examples below, bear in mind that they are only guidelines; you must take into account your own instincts and knowledge of your own situation.

The "A"

A basic feature of type "A" is that you usually see him only when it is convenient for him, never on Sundays and rarely on holidays, and may not hear from him for several days running. Or if perchance you do see him fairly often, he has doubtless told you time and again that he is leaving his wife "soon," but you have been eminently unsuccessful, during the five or more years he has been monopolizing your time, in pinning down "when." Though he tells you his marriage is on the rocks, he's still never able to spend a night away from home, shies away from taking you to certain places for fear of being seen, and never gives you any money that he couldn't account for.

One friend of mine, who deserved a booby prize for her naiveté with men, had an "A" type worth citing. Very much married, with two lovely children, this "A" also had a penchant for "anything in skirts," as they used to say (which today I presume would be "anything in jeans").

"A" 's confession to my friend was that he no longer had any physical contact with his wife, that it was impossible to relate to her on any other level because she had not "grown" with him, and that, moreover, she was completely frigid. (He would never have married her in the first place had she not become pregnant was his final admission.)

By Christmas, six months after the affair began, though it was impossible for them to be together because of "the children," love still reigned supreme, and my friend, who will be henceforth known as "Poor Darling," gave "A" an expensive gift from Tiffany's. I am unable to remember his gift to her but it was definitely not in the Tiffany league. Kresge's would be closer. Around Easter she found out that the wife to whom he could not relate, she of the stunted development, frigid nature, and marriage by reason of pregnancy only, was expecting another blessed bundle.

Poor Darling was distraught. She refused to see him, showed manifestations of shattered nerves, and had to seek the counsel of doctor, psychologist, and friends. But when he finally reached her with a "satisfactory" explanation, all was again sweetness and light—whenever he wanted it to be and could find the time. (In case you haven't guessed, his "satisfactory" explanation was that his wife's pregnancy was a "fluke," the result of his despondency one night over Poor Darling's threat to stop seeing him—after he had failed to keep three dates in a row. His wife was so comforting and supportive that particular night that, without warning, "it" just happened.)

The last I heard, two or three years later, "it" was still happening between "A" and Poor Darling.

In addition to the qualifications already described, "A"s frequently display at least three of the following features: *

* In the following type-patterns the attentive reader will note, hopefully with dismay, a constant shift from the collective "they" to the individual

1. They have considerable financial holdings in conjunction with their wives (they have recently bought and newly furnished a home in the suburbs; for tax purposes her name was included on the incorporating papers of his firm; or he runs the family business for *her* father).

2. They have two or three (or more) children, his salary is small, and he is already in debt over his head.

3. They have already been divorced once before and are still saddled with alimony or child support to a former wife.

4. They warn you indirectly that you can expect only rejection from them because, although they keep saying "soon," you realize, after five years, that "soon" really means "never."

5. They lied about being married when you met. (One woman, suspicious about never being able to call her "boy friend" or see him on certain occasions, nonetheless accepted his story that he was obliged to take in his elderly mother, whom he was loath to institutionalize, and did not like to disturb her with calls, or leave her alone too often. Only when an emergency arose and she was forced to call him did she find that the lady she apologized to for disturbing had been miraculously transformed from feeble mother to vigorous and interrogating wife.)

6. They are recently married and prone to phoning home frequently in your company. Or, conversely, they have been married ten years or more and the marriage shows no signs of cracking.

7. They are public figures who can *never* take you out in public for fear of being seen and "making the columns."

8. They can somehow afford all luxuries for himself and the "little lady," but nothing for you.

"he." When queried about this, I realized that turning specific instances into major generalizations is just one of many quirks of the self-defeating. It may not be grammatic, but it sure is neurotic.

The "B"

Men in this category are only slightly less impossible than the "A" variety and may share certain of their qualifications (complicated financial arrangements with their wives, dependent children, small income, etc.). However, there are certain indications that the man in question likes you somewhat better than his "A" fellow deceiver does. For example, he may contribute to your support; or even maintain you entirely and have a key to your apartment (of course expecting to find you there whenever he barges in unannounced). Or you may see him on a schedule that affords rejection you can look forward to: Tuesday evening for dinner and a "quickie" dessert at your place before he has to rush home before curfew, and Saturday morning at the crack of dawn when he comes in donned in golf attire, ready to tee off before you can pry your other eye open.

A "B" may introduce you to family friends, or even take you to his house when his wife's away, supposedly to show how much he likes you.

Or your heart throb in the "B" group may take you out to great places, declare his undying love, but cheat on you as much as he does on his wife. (One holiday when he stood you up you had a male friend phone his house to find that his wife had not seen him either.)

The "C"

Men in this classification are in a marriage that is obviously on the rocks, not only from what they say but from what you see. They spend most of their time with you, including holidays, and they may even have suggested leaving their wife to come live with you. But, alas, not a word of marriage. Or if perchance they have mentioned marriage, it was only to declare that they have *had* it and know that no "piece of paper" can mean happiness for two people. But you are dying to marry in white, have contributed to shower gifts for five years in your office, and are straining at the bit to "collect" what you are owed. Or maybe your godfather is a minister and you have promised him he could perform the ceremony as soon as there is one, and it would be impossible to "pretend" that you were married.

Imagine the fun you can have suffering with this *hombre*. (In fact, the whole experience could be even more frustrating than with one of the "A" or "B" types, because "C" has shown that he does care for you.) If you use your head with this one, you can hassle him so much about marrying you that you may even begin to make his wife look good to him and send him scurrying back to her.

Isn't the thought of *that* possibility almost too good to bear?

The "D"

The "D" type almost miss the wrong-man classification because, although married, he has already left home and asked your hand in marriage, the moment he is free—which could be never, for his wife has vowed to get "messy" should he seek a divorce; she'll name you corespondent and give other details that could adversely affect his sensitive political career or corporate image for life.

The "E"

The "E" category consists of men already in the process of divorce (whose papers you have actually seen), who are firmly planning to remarry (perhaps even making deposits in your bank account in preparation) and devotedly seeing you on a regular basis. Consequently, I do not find them worth discussing at any length. However, if you manage to become involved with someone of this ilk, you'd better do your homework on alienation procedures and techniques (as outlined in other sections of this book), for the very fact of his being married may lull you into a false sense of security. For that reason alone you have to be especially wary of "E."

Operation Salvage

Another sure-fire way to select a wrong man (and waste valuable time) is what I call "operation salvage," which involves extensive renovation of an obviously objectionable prospect, or one unmistakably below par. The idea is to choose someone on the basis of what you might remold him into rather than on what you have to begin with. Try to find a target as far removed from the one you have in mind as possible. And make sure that the alterations you plan center around those features of his personality, or aspects of his life, that appear to be most basic to his nature. Or simply most enjoyable to him. Here are a few examples on which to model your conduct.

The 100-Proof Project

This project is recommended especially for women who hate heavy drinkers and loathe people lacking in will power. You are not apt to find a better renovation project than this, or one more apt to collapse around you in the end, once you have enjoyed all the rejection income from it that you can take.

The object is an alcoholic who, you realize within the first few minutes of meeting him, is under the influence. Establish in your own mind that his drinking represents a problem; then decide that you can "work with" or reform him. The moment you start going out with him, begin your nagging, or "work." Lecture him on the deleterious effects of alcohol, sermonize about the importance of resolve, berate him about not working steady, and otherwise try to help him. In this way you can incur his wrath and set yourself up for hostile responses, rejection, and "get-even" abuse.

Forty cups of black coffee, thirty-three disappointments, and countless quarrels later, when he comes up with a new job and goes (temporarily) off the sauce, take an "objective" look at him. Notice how attractive, charming, and alert—in comparison—he can be. Think about his good points: he doesn't gamble, he's tall enough for you, he drinks only Thursday through Monday, and he still looks attractive (like a darling tousled boy who lacks only good care)—and realize that you are in love! Or, if you are less romantic, remind yourself as a practical matter that there are not many single men around, and since there is less competition for him (understandably) you'd better concentrate on this prospect if you ever want to get married (which you don't).

Now that your future plans depend on him, extract a firm promise from him that he will never drink again. This will give you the opportunity to have a giant fight the next time he appears, shortly thereafter, in his usual state.

Begin sending for literature from Alcoholics Anonymous with his return address. Weepingly—or bullyingly—prevail on him to attend meetings of AA or similar organizations with you. Then, during question-and-answer periods, ask questions that reveal personal, embarrassing problems of his, so that he will feel too self-conscious to return and possibly be helped. Say, "What can a woman do when alcohol makes her boy friend impotent?" Or, "What's the best product to take pee out of the rug?"

Question friends and relatives—yours and his—whether they know a hypnotist or psychiatrist who could deal effectively with his situation. Confide in them the trials and tribulations that beset you because you (willingly) chose him.

Of course, the more you harass him, the more he'll drink, the more hostile he will become, and soon he will start standing you up, abusing and rejecting you even more than usual. Or when he does show you'll wish he hadn't, since he drinks so much he winds up at the end of the evening a dead weight, a crumpled carcass on the sofa, impossible to budge. Or he may simply fall down in front of your family or friends—the ultimate (self-willed) embarrassment.

Now decide that the situation is intolerable and vow never to see him again; hang up when he calls and instruct anyone who might get his call at work to say you are not in. However, when he meets you after work all spruced up and respectably sober, take up the project where you left off.

When he begins drinking again more than ever—even on Tuesdays and Wednesdays—and after several fights (over your trying to keep his car keys, hide or water down his [bottled] spirits), conclude, along with some doctors, that the illness is basically physical. Decide that it is all due to a chemical imbalance and embrace various and sundry theories on how this should be corrected. For example, on the theory that it is due to a vitamin deficiency, ply him with vitamins. Or when it appears that the problem is more complex, incorporate the "an alcoholic is only thirsty" theory and flood him with soft drinks *with* the vitamins (as he angrily protests he is not really an alcoholic).

If by some miraculous misfortune you stumble on an approach that can and does cure him—making the project a total loss—you will of course have to start prospecting for another model. But if you're careful to hook up with a real honest-to-God lush, your chances for curing your model are minimal. I've known this "100-proof project" to supply ongoing rejection bliss for months on end, sometimes years. (Added bonus: black-and-blue spots if your target turns violent when off the wagon.)

Drug Addicts

It has been found that among certain discriminating masochists the pain threshold is so high that it is virtually impossible to gratify them. In such cases, when a cat-o'-nine-tails would produce but a titillating tingle, an affair with a mere alcoholic would leave the subject still unsatiated and panting for more. If you happen to belong to this select group, you might want to consider an affair with a drug addict. As with the alcoholic, the ploy is to believe he can be salvaged.

The Junkie (or "H" Is for Hell)

While many think the use of drugs is on the wane today, anyone who sets her mind to it can doubtless find an addict. If the idea of becoming involved with a junkie strikes you as glaringly self-destructive, you may prefer to close your eyes to the fact that he was "strung out" when you met. When the evidence becomes too apparent to deny, you can always think about the times a "good woman" has "saved" a seemingly destroyed man. (Though you must naturally overlook the much more frequent incidences in which a woman was dragged down the drain by such a person.) Identifying with him because of your own suffering, conclude passionately—and correctly—that *someone* must help him. Remember, too, that you will be *needed* by an addict, and that if you can help him recover he will (theoretically) be indebted to you for life. But, most important of all, constantly keep in mind that no one better would really want to stay with you anyway.

Because of the desperation and frustration it assures, not to mention the tremendous daily expense and the low percentage of cures, involvement with a heroin junkie has to be recommended over involvement with all other addicts.

One of the first things you are apt to notice about a heroin addict is his "cool" manner . . . nonchalance . . .

drawn-out speech pattern—yeaahhh! Look for the shades he will wear to protect his eyes from the excessive light his dilated pupils would otherwise let in. Depending on the stage of his addiction and the time you meet him, he may be so "relaxed" he will appear to be nodding off to sleep. (He will explain that he hasn't been to bed in two nights.) In addition, notice how he brushes his nose repeatedly and at times does a Napoleon scratch, inside his shirt or elsewhere—this, as with all his movements, will be in slow motion, which you can still define as "cool": "Like, what's the rush, man?" Adding to his contained manner will be the fact that, unlike most men, he will not be trying to whisk you off to the first available bed. That in itself—the fact that junkies don't generally like sex—offers frustration possibilities not to be underestimated.

Another symptom of the drug addict is his phenomenal ability to concoct lies and master the art of deception and complete unreliability, which will provide much of the misery you can anticipate enjoying. The big lie will usually start when you discover he is on drugs, or finally get him to admit it. At this juncture he will usually have a tall but very touching story to explain how he got on drugs in 'Nam. Naturally, it would be positively unpatriotic not to try to "save this poor veteran and victim of circumstances" . . . even though he probably never set foot in Vietnam.

Once you are seriously involved with an addict, you can expect to be stood up and frustrated continually. If you are expecting him on Monday he may not appear until Thursday, and then looking incredibly disheveled and seedy. If he swears on his father's grave that he is going to get into a rehabilitation program, often after you have made twenty calls to various agencies and prevailed on someone you know to intervene for him, he will almost surely not keep the appointment and not be seen or heard from for a week. Or, trembling and sobbing and pouring out his heart about how he wants to stop taking drugs, he may tell you about a program he could get into or a doctor who is supposed to have a system for curing addicts. And, adding that he doesn't want to end up in jail or dead on some rooftop in his own filth, he may beg you for money to start the climb back up. (Your addict will, of course, be sufficiently attractive to make you believe that he could be a good catch, if only he could get off dope.)

If you give him the money he asks for, however, he will not be seen or heard from until it is gone. And should you buy him clothes or otherwise try to make him look decent, they will be on his back but a short time before they will wind up converted to dope—for his arm.

When you stop giving him money, he will consider your action an invitation to steal. Moreover, your refusal to give him money could, as with the lush, result in violence. You lucky girl!

When you have finally had enough and flatly refuse to see him, he will probably—to punish you and get a rest—wind up in jail. When he gets out, having gained twenty pounds (more handsome than you believed possible), and comes claiming to have a good job offer and talking marriage, saying he can't see how he ever got mixed up in drugs in the first place, realize how much you really love him. Show him you have confidence in him by giving him your key. And two weeks later, when you catch him nodding out, believe him when he swears he's clean and is only taking tranquilizers on the doctor's orders during this "transitional" period. Shortly after this, when you return home to find everything of value missing, including him, you may decide you have had enough of a junkie. Or will you?

The Pill Poppers

Since many of you may never have the opportunity to meet a real live heroin addict, it's good to know a bit about the barbiturate and amphetamine addicts. Although this habit is less expensive and less devastating, its effects still offer a gold mine of potential rejection and frustration.

Since barbiturates are a depressant to the central nervous system, like heroin they dull a person's senses and slow his movements. You will also notice that the barbiturate addict seems poorly coordinated, the drug having affected his equilibrium. (He may sometimes be mistaken for a drunk.) In addition, the barbiturate addict may have an exaggerated sense of his own importance (or, conversely, feel very insecure); or he may smile, seemingly to himself, or during conversations when a smile does not appear indicated. Since this drug interferes with the natural sleep pattern, his sleep is often fitful, and he may wake up screaming or talking erratically. A seriously addicted man could die if he discontinued the drug's use abruptly. (Of course, someone hooked on downers, like those addicted to any other drug, will always claim that he can "stop any time he pleases.") In addition, since barbiturate toxins build up in the system, with time a dangerous and in some cases fatal accumulation can poison the individual and result in death, as can the mixture of barbiturates with alcohol.

However, concentrating on such isolated and generally impertinent facts that two wealthy, self-admitted pill addicts and country singers have reformed to make a useful life, decide that there is hope for your affair after all. Remind yourself that his basic credentials are presentable with this one small exception and that no one is perfect. Then fasten your seat belt.

Amphetamine addiction begins innocently enough in most cases—taking "pep pills" to stay awake to study for exams, to complete an important job project, make a long road trip, lose weight (sometimes by a doctor's prescription), or fit in at a party. But before long one pill won't do it, and while two can, three or four are better. And up and up it goes, to keep "up," to provide the invigorating sensation that all is beautiful, and I-can-do-it-better-now self-assurance. (The latter applies to everything from having sex or playing a musical instrument to composing a literary work, but is often based on chemical illusion only.)

About eight years ago I had my first encounter with a Speedy P.P. in the flesh, and certainly my first impression of him was favorable. His manner was animated and high spirited (though as I reflect on it, a bit spastic), and he was stimulating and witty. His conversation was fascinating as he exhibited an ability to talk about anything and everything—sometimes, it seemed, simultaneously. Despite all this, and even the fact that his shirttail needed tucking in on one side, his tie was askew, and he had a habit of biting his lip, he attracted me, moth-to-flame style.

But as he began to discuss his research project, his personality seemed to change markedly. He became sullen and morose, especially as he discussed his partner, who he felt was not sufficiently dedicated (he seemed prepared to work through the night without stopping while his partner became exhausted, and his partner had come to question his judgment in certain serious ways, or not understand him without considerable repetition of what he regarded as simple deductions).

All these warning signals were as sweet invitations to me. If he were a more likely and less obviously flawed prospect, I would have been competing with him for every breath of silent air, and otherwise practicing master-stroke techniques to alienate him, but in this case I was the perfect listener. In addition to urging him to talk about his project, a superfluous gesture as it turned out, my prevailing thought was on ways I might soothe and relax him once we became better friends.

All my efforts were in vain, however, for as he went on about his project at a clipped pace and I began to find it more and more difficult to follow, he began to appear distracted. The next thing I knew, not simply in the middle of the conversation but in the middle of a sentence (shortly after he had asked himself a question and then answered it), he got up and left—not only my presence but the party.

Not long after this I heard that he was fighting dismissal from his teaching post (he claimed that it was a personal vendetta).

It did not occur to me that he was addicted to amphetamines, simply because my concept of a drug addict at that time was more stereotyped. However, by the time he finally turned up a few years later and called me as if we had spoken only the day before, I had heard about his drug problem. Nevertheless, I invited him over for dinner. (Even then I knew the value of cluttering one's life up with people who could never serve any useful purpose but get in the way of more likely prospects. See "The Clutterers" for further details.)

When he arrived, it was difficult to believe he was the same person. He seemed a scarecrow, on which ill-fitting clothes hung loosely. His hair had fallen out, in an irregular pattern of bald spots, and some of his teeth were missing. He spoke freely about his drug problem, explained his plan to stop using the pills, but added that he was unable to accomplish anything, even getting up in the morning without them. He trembled, sometimes ground his teeth, and repeatedly changed subjects in the midst of a thought. He was as tragic a figure as I have ever seen—so tragic, in fact, that he was no longer even useful as a rejection-fulfillment target.

The No-Win Big Gamble

The rejection stakes here are so high that women who may be otherwise conservative daringly throw their hearts out like chips, to be wagered at 1000-to-1 odds—against their winning. And while the suffering is not as severe as in trying to reform an addict, it is so dependable and sustained that it can nevertheless provide great fulfillment.

All you have to do is find a compulsive gambler (if possible, one who has already lost at least one wife, his family, dog, three cars, eight jobs, and a couple of businesses, all because of his "sport"). Be sure he tells you that he has had enough and is going to stop as soon as he wins a bundle on the Preakness. Hopefully, he may have a bad case of "the shorts" when you meet him and will be obliged to put the touch on you from time to time (or even constantly). Should you meet him at a time when he is temporarily in the money, just bide your time; he will soon be "out" and will shortly settle back into his "natural" state of financial desperation.

When you set out to reform your gamblin' man, show how understanding you are by accompanying him to his usual haunts. For example, go with him to the races, and when it is apparent his juices are really flowing at the promising possibility of losing his rent money, calmly point out the odds against his winning. Explain to him that, according to a psychiatrist friend of yours, he doesn't *want* to win and is only out to punish himself by losing. Explain, too, how he is hurting himself and all those around him—which will only encourage him to add the phone-bill money to the gambling pot.

Or go with him to a party at which most of the men disappear into a back room early in the evening and are not heard from again till well past midnight. By then, when he is probably desperately trying to recoup his losses (or lose everything he has already won), walk into the room and ask him to take you home. If he refuses, remind him how much he has already lost in his lifetime, perhaps starting an argument and making a scene.

After it becomes obvious to him that you are not fit to take out into polite (gambling) society, your social life will wither to dust as BG repeatedly breaks dates because he got so involved in a little game that he didn't know what time it was, or lost all the money he had intended to take you out with. The more you lecture him, the more resentful he will become, which in turn will make him even more inclined to stand you up.

During discouraging times, when for instance he might

come over in a rumpled suit that looks as if he had slept in it, and a three-day growth of beard, consider his good side. He doesn't have any other vices—boozing, chasing women, etc. He has an easygoing personality (though he may have ulcers and his nails are bitten down to the quick), and he rarely tells you no (preferring to disappoint you when you find he did not do what you had asked).

After a particularly bad run of luck, during which he not only reclaims the watch he gave you for Christmas to pawn but talks you out of any other other valuables you may have, and proposes that you borrow a substantial sum of money from your elderly parents, send him to hell in no uncertain terms. However, after a few weeks have gone by, and you have met a more likely prospect whom you find utterly boring, relent and let BG back in. You might even want to reconsider his loan request in view of how much you found you've missed him (making you miserable), and given the fact that you have already made so much of an investment of time, energy, tears, and money in him.

Whatever your reasons for wanting to become involved with this tempting target, always pretending there is a possibility you can effect a real change, you should be able to get years of suffering out of this one if you play your cards right.

The Homosexual Reconversion Project

If you are hopelessly project-oriented (calling the projects "challenging") and unable to manage one with an alcoholic, drug addict, or gambler, try a homosexual. Not only will you delight in many fruitless months of almost guaranteed wasted effort, trying to convert the man in question *after* you have isolated the problem; you can also waste considerable time before, pretending not to recognize that a complete overhaul is in order. The man in this plan, often well turned out, gainfully employed, creative, and

—most important—unmarried, gives a girl every justification for resolving to reconstruct the one incidental feature that needs a slight adjustment: he prefers men.

An industrious, talented, and fashionable friend of mine who managed to be involved in three of these projects in recent years served as one of my consultants for making up the following blueprint. She explained that her preference for stylish, attractive men with imagination, who also seemed to take a special interest in her fashion image, resulted in her relationships with homosexuals. Of course, while most of us would find such a person interesting, her desire to try to possess, dominate, and convert such men was the one essential for her (and your) success in this area.

When you first meet your prospect, you may feel an immediate affinity. He proves to be very knowledgeable about woman's doings, and when he invites you out he sometimes has constructive comments to make about exciting changes you could make in your fashion image. Some types may offer to accompany you on a shopping trip, and linger behind, pulling, tugging, and examining the articles of feminine apparel after you are more than ready to leave. They are also concerned about their own fashion image, and you may have to compete with them for a place in the mirror.

If there is another attractive man around, your prospect does not appear the least jealous of you. In fact, he may pay you very little attention but be especially witty and charming, appearing as anxious as you are to make a favorable impression. Indeed, he may offer to drop someone off one evening and take you home first.

When doubts begin to arise about his rather unconventional behavior, and, especially, should you finally meet the male friend to whom he frequently refers, only to receive an icy stare and inquisitive once-over, reluctantly suspect the truth. But begin to concentrate on his good points or redeeming features: He is understanding, thoughtful, respectful. He has never tried to make a pass at you, perhaps because, unlike most of the others, he holds you in such high regard he does not want to cheapen the relationship with some shoddy proposal of unsanctified passion.

Call to mind any brush with romance you may have had with him, perhaps remembering the time when, in his exuberance over the way some recipe turned out, he kissed you on the tip of the nose.

Whenever you have a free moment, think how wonderful it will be when he finally holds you in his arms and declares the love he obviously feels (why else would he have bothered to select that beautiful ensemble for you?). Concoct an imaginary love scene between you. Try to think of him when you lie down to sleep, perchance to dream.

By this time, he has become important to you, so you can accept the truth but you cannot abandon him. He needs you—needs your help. Remember what the psychiatrist on the radio said: every man desires a normal relationship with a woman, but many are unable to find one, usually because of fears of inadequacy. (Ignore any psychiatric views to the contrary.)

Oversimplify the problem so that it boils down to building up his self-confidence, being understanding and patient (wasting more time). Meanwhile, consider the positive side: You do not have to worry about other women. You are needed. You can feel superior on this score because he is "sick" and you are not—much!

Launch a program to boost his self-confidence and demonstrate your respect for his masculinity. Request his opinion when you need a male point of view. Ask him to move furniture, or to carry packages that are too heavy for you, or to remove tight bottle caps. Divert the conversation to questions on sports and other topics that should (but obviously do not) appeal to him.

In the second stage of the program, if he has not been

undone by the first, warm up to him gradually. Although he has never made a pass at you, and may indeed have disappeared for several days after you suggested that you might be receptive to one, conclude that his burning, secret desire is to have a full-blown romance with you.

Try to arrange to see him more frequently so there will be less time for him—and, not incidentally, you—to see others.

Limited by rules of decorum and convention from making overt romantic gestures, use the subtle ones to appeal to his basic romantic instincts. Keep your hand on his a little longer than necessary when making some point, or hold onto his arm after having safely crossed the street. If you do not see him for a few days, tell him you missed him.

Moving from warm to warmer, "accidentally" select a movie or theater production described in reviews as having an emphasis on sex. Afterward, pretending to be shocked by it all, ask his opinion of certain scenes. This will break the ice and permit an opening into the area he has avoided thus far. (Unlike the weather, once you start talking about *this* subject, doing something about it is in order.)

Make him uncomfortable by complimenting him on his eyes, or mouth, or physique. If you do not mind possibly causing him to perspire, mention his teeth, or something about his mouth, with a clear implication that you would not resent his pressing it against yours. Such an implied invitation is about as welcome as a hint to a nonswimmer that he go take a jump in the lake.

When you are ready to move into high gear, try to awaken his natural instincts by wearing something particularly feminine (in case he had not noticed) the next time he comes over. Have the usual seventy-five-watt bulb subtly replaced by a twenty-five-watter. Confess that you like him very much (perhaps even take his hand; is it moist?). Try to evoke some declaration from him; ask him boldly if he likes you too, and similar embarrassing questions.

When he finally escapes from these and other tender traps designed to touch emotions far too deep for you to reach with your naive and ineffectual techniques, he will be careful to avoid coming again within your reach.

After he fails to call the next day, the next, and so on for several more, call *him* and candidly discuss his problem, stressing your understanding and sympathetic attitude toward it. Suggest that the answer may be to see a psychiatrist, although he probably has been seeing one for years and may well be thinking *you* need to see one if you are still unable to understand the completely different kind of friendship he wanted with you.

Reading Between the Lines
(*How to Recognize the Gay Deceivers and Lucky Pierres*)

You have already seen how much valuable time can be lost, and sweet rejection gained, in trying to convert a recognizable, committed homosexual friend. (My sister's analogy of such projects is "trying to make a shoe serve as a hat.") Here is a similar project that promises even greater rejection rewards, protection against marriage, and a real treat for the more neurotic among you.

This involves becoming engaged in a relationship with the part-time homosexual who, unlike those who accept their sexual inclination, tries to deny and fight it, often by overcompensating with women. Sometimes known as the Gay Deceivers or Lucky Pierres (the latter because of their ability to go either way), they are usually guilt-stricken and resentful of themselves, and consequently contemptuous of any woman so undiscriminating as to want them.

The only problem is that since most GD and LP activity is "undercover," it is not always possible to get the right reading on them (particularly since the map does not represent the "territory"). Therefore, your first effort should be to learn how to read between the lines, to recognize your subjects by their attitudes, preferences, habits, actions, and various features of their lifestyles. Some of the signs you should look for are:

Big Displays, Empty Boxes

Because of the desire of closet homosexuals (or even those suppressing homosexual tendencies) to disguise their true inclinations, many of them make a career of demonstrating how mad they are about girls and posing as great lovers. They continually make a great public display of their passionate nature. When the moment of truth arrives, of course, and it is time to actually inspect the merchandise that they have been touting, more often than not one finds only empty boxes or what one of my more knowledgeable researchers has dubbed the CGU syndrome.*

A typical example of the BDEB type, who always sells more than he can deliver, can often be found in the party scene. For it is there that he is in his glory—pinching, squeezing, patting, and clawing at every fanny not protected by an overstuffed chair, or any pair of knockers not guarded by a male security force. His verbal assault is no more subtle, and he is sometimes so explicit about what he would like to do (and how), so embarrassingly aggressive, that it is awkward for many girls to accept his invitation even if so inclined (a rejection he subconsciously welcomes).

But if someone wants to buy the "hard" sell, the whole picture suddenly changes. For, after having touted his masculinity in public, in private he becomes quite reticent, often moody and sullen, or excessively critical. Also, many BDEB types have drinking problems, and drink so much prior to the moment they are to submit their wares for testing that they can hardly speak coherently, much

* From the Latin *cantgetitup* witha derrickstarchn'splint.

less function sexually. (Besides drinking too much, to have an excuse for their inability to perform, many members of this species drink to escape feelings of guilt, to excuse "what happened that night.")

The Perennial Conquistadores
(The Don Juan Syndrome)

If any of you are under the mistaken impression that I think *all* big-display boys feature empty boxes, quickly disabuse yourself of this idea. Unlike the empty boxers, the PCs often feature not only one sterling performance but sometimes three or four (or one sustained production as long as three or four); their only difficulty may be in having a climax.

Since they are such powerful lovers, and frequently attractive in general, they have girls wall-to-wall, sometimes changing practically every night, and enjoy the reputation far and wide of great lovers and playboys.

However, as most psychiatrists long ago observed, the classic Don Juan, who is supposed to be in love with all women, is often not in love with any. But, wishing to fight his innate attraction to men, he energetically conducts a search for the "right" girl—propositioning, loving, and leaving all others by the score.

If he happens to find someone who appears to be Ms. Right, he will lavish his attentions on her, admitting the excesses of the past but vowing (sometimes convincingly) that it will be different this time. Nevertheless, before long Ms. usually begins to hear reports of Mr. having been seen with someone else—sometimes shortly after having taken her home. Or that he is desperately trying to get the telephone number of a ravishing new girl around town, or even of her best friend. (He will leave no stone unturned, looking for his ideal woman—who just may turn out to be a man.)

As you can see, the likelihood of your effecting an ongoing relationship with someone in this category is rather remote, since the mark of the Perennial Conquistador is to "love and leave." Still, what you may lose here in the area of sustained rejection fulfillment may be partially compensated for by the intensity of the moment.

Gymnasium Jim

Although a certain concern for keeping in shape shows a healthy degree of self-esteem, when a man's entire preoccupation is with barbells, pushups, punching bags, and nothing deeper than a rippling muscle, you may just have a gay deceiver under the brawn. Here are some things to watch for:

• Do too graceful hand movements sometimes stand out in contrast to the muscular arm?

• Does his conversation sometimes suggest that he is a reluctant dragon in matters of sex because this could interfere with his body-building program?

• Does he frequently strike poses as if waiting for Rodin to surface and sculpt him?

• Though he may not usually drink, when he takes one too many does he begin to fawn over his fellow man as if he is interested in participating in a mutual muscle study in cozier quarters?

• Does he wear caressingly fitted casual pants and sweaters and take an hour before the mirror to effect his carefree air (possibly changing several times)?

• Does he generously share his vital statistics at the drop of a weight?

• Does he frequently tell tales about girls who try to pick him up to no avail?

• Are his buddies all fellow musclemen whose current conversation about "working out" refers strictly to doing it in the gym?

The Hostility Act

This type constantly seeks to embarrass any woman he's involved with, especially in the presence of others, attacking her lack of intelligence (calling her stupid, a dumb broad, etc.), revealing embarrassing personal details (age, etc.), criticizing her appearance (even slight overweight, etc.).

He never has anything good to say about women, and, besides always echoing the common clichés ("Women talk too much," "Women are vicious, can't be trusted," "Women are extravagant," "Women are too emotional to hold certain positions," etc.), he frequently voices the more vicious ones. You'll be able to recognize this type, too, by his almost inevitable put-down of "gays," whom at some point he'll manage to work into the conversation and then work over. In my experience, he'll generally tell how some "fairy" tried to "make him," which will be followed by the equally inevitable happy ending, or how Mr. Hostile managed to fend off the offender and keep his honor intact. I've always found these stories especially strange, since this type's open contempt for "gays," detectable at a hundred paces, would keep even the boldest homosexuals from wanting to approach him.

While we could go on at length about the reasons for such an attitude, for our purposes the point is that for the truly neurotic woman such male hostility is a potential gold mine, and should be exploited without a moment's hesitation.

The Practicing "Man's Man"

Although to designate someone as a "man's man" usually means that he is respected and admired by men, when a man gets to be so much of a man's man that it is virtually impossible to separate him from the boys, you'd better check him out. He may just be a fine rejection target. Here are some of the telltale signs to watch for.

1. He is an active member of numerous all-male clubs, lodges, sports teams, etc., that occupy practically all his time, and when he has a free moment, most of his conversation centers around the activities of such groups.

2. Almost all reminiscences about fun-filled times in the past exclude any mention of girls.

3. Vacations and out-of-town trips are usually with his buddies, and in general he seems to prefer spending considerable money with them to minimal amounts with you.

4. At parties, he generally gravitates to the cluster of men, where conversations are on cigars, sports cars, sports (varying only with the seasons), and sex (with emphasis on how many times he balled this chick, or laid another).

While again we will leave psychiatric speculation about this type to those more competent than we, we do want to stress the potential wealth here for any reasonably neurotic woman. And if ever you feel uncomfortable for any reason about becoming involved with a lush, a gambler, a drug addict, or any other types whose public conduct could redound to your discredit, remember that the "man's man" offers you the possibility of being the envy of friend and foe alike. For on the outside at least your target will appear everything a girl ever dreamed of wanting, while inside he doubtless offers as many rejection possibilities as you're liable to encounter in a month of Sundays.

Operation Occupational Counseling

In your search for wrong-man types you do not have to limit yourself to the most obvious ones. For example, you could choose a nongambling, nondrinking heterosexual who works, say, as a clerk in an important brokerage house. Mr. Clerk would still fall very much into the wrong-man category if what you really want is a top-echelon executive and are determined to make your clerk attain this station.

When you meet someone you feel sure you can prod, push, or guide to greater heights, begin by trying to improve his image of himself, assuring him that he is much too good for the position he currently holds. Question him about the higher positions in his firm and mentally select one for him (though he may have been with the company only a short time or there may be many people far ahead of him in line for the position in mind). Subtly remind him of the old "behind every great man there's a woman" theme and say that the only reason he is not further ahead is because he has never before received the right encouragement.

When he seems to accept your argument, tell him the first thing he needs is a new wardrobe befitting his new position (which he does not yet have, just as he does not have the income that goes with it). Point out that if he thinks small he will never be big, and when you have convinced him you are right, go with him on a shopping tour. In the store, discourse with the salesman about the proper style, color, and cut for your target. Veto anything you consider inappropriate, even if he is under the impression that he knows exactly what he wants.

Once you are satisfied with his new business image, take up the actual career aspects of your project.

Familiarize yourself with the duties and systems involved in his work and suggest immediate and radical reorganization. If the routine of a fellow employee is disrupted by the change, the plan is especially advisable.

Impress on him the importance of going out of the way to accommodate the boss's wife whenever she calls or comes in. Brush aside his explanation that his normal duties do not bring him into contact with her, or his admonitions that the boss seems to be the jealous type.

Badger him about enrolling in evening courses at the university. Disregard the possible fact that he detests school and was never a good student, or that your job-improvement program keeps him fully occupied getting up an hour earlier to be waiting outside when the boss arrives, and working overtime—without pay—every evening.

After you have given him these constructive suggestions, seek daily reports on his progress. Question him about the boss's response to his new efforts, prevailing on him to interpret morning greetings. Say, "Did he sound happier with you? Is he friendlier than before?" Try to guess how long it will be before he will be elevated to the coveted position. If he does not advance as quickly as you think he should, react as if you believed it to be a deliberate betrayal—of you by him.

Before too long this ungrateful wretch will decide that, even if he cannot advance from his present lowly position, he would prefer to exist in peace. This will make it necessary for him to resign—from your company.

Converting an Introvert

If your particular form of neurotic behavior leans toward hyperarticulation, logorrhea, or other kinds of extroversion, you ought to consider looking for a quiet man in order to "bring him out." Obviously, all he needs to mend his ways is a happy-go-lucky, outgoing woman.

One of the first things you should do after meeting such a target is to guide him into a situation where his conversational deficiency is sure to stand out. Then—with everyone listening for the answer—ask him why he is always so quiet. Afterward, give him a little speech on all the "profound" things he already knows: there is no reason to be shy around others (who are, after all, only harmless human beings like him); he is as intelligent as many, more so than most of those who talk incessantly, but people will never find that out if he never speaks up.

The next time you see him, give him a book on self-projection, the art of self-expression, or how to mix.* Recommend that he take a course in public speaking, or personality development, or even salesmanship, telling him that he has got to learn to sell *himself* more. If you want to

---

* One of the best on the subject is Dr. Naomi Nussbaum's 800-page tome: *Four Hundred Twenty Lessons to a Better Personality in Ten Days or Less.*

delay your inevitable rejection by him and seem slightly less obnoxious, cite the positive things he has to offer or sell, telling him how ridiculous it is to act as if he were ashamed to be alive.

To test his progress (especially if he seems embarrassed because of his inability to relate better to others), the next time you go out with him, attribute to him some controversial point of view he has discussed with you in private, forcing him to try to defend it. Say, "Herbie here thinks Nixon was clean as a hound's tooth." Or, after centering the conversation around him by quoting clever little things he has done or said, urge him to tell everyone about the night a certain thing happened (make it intimate). If he's the man I think he is, he will stutter, stumble, and get everything backward in his self-conscious confusion. (Justify your conduct by convincing yourself that this will force him to improve his delivery.)

Find ways to shove him into the spotlight, front and center, where he is clearly most uncomfortable. Reject any suggestion on his part that the two of you have a quiet dinner somewhere or engage in activity where he can relax offstage, away from the madding crowd.

Soon, no matter how much he may have liked you—perhaps attracted to your more outgoing personality—he will realize that, reluctant performer that he is, the last thing he needs is to be constantly shoved front and center stage, and the next thing you know he will have bowed out.

Secondary (but Important) Wrong-Man Types

There are certain other wrong-man types that you can recognize quickly with only a few leads and clues. They are sometimes known as the Old Dependables because of the reliable record of rejection that girls have been able to stack up with them.

Mama's Boy Roy: If you meet someone over thirty who,

though financially secure, is still living at home, he is probably a great prospect for the MBR category. If you see such signs of apron-string entanglement as refusal to eat out (preferring Mama's food), frequent references to Mother's dependence on him, canceled dates for reasons involving her, complaints about her attempts to dominate him while nonetheless refusing to leave home, you've probably found dream-boy Roy, whose heart (and soul) belong to Mama.

Job-Jumping John: If in your first conversation he alludes to the three jobs he has had in the past six months, know that you're immediately on the track of something good. If you meet him between jobs and he begins philosophizing about the inequities of a system in which a person is robbed of his time for eight hours a day but must submit to exist, you can be sure you have struck pay dirt. Remember, there is no rejection quite so gratifying as that repeatedly supplied by someone you are supporting financially, and, while he may judge it a major crime that he be required to work, he probably wouldn't consider it a misdemeanor to sponge off you while *you* work.

Lying Larry: If you catch him in repeated lies and conclude he is a pathological liar, decide that the one time he is telling the truth is when he says he loves you or wants to marry you. Stake your hopes on elaborate plans he envisions, sharing them with your friends so that when everything fails to materialize, you can doubly enjoy the humiliation.

Perennial-Bachelor Bob: Bachelor Bobs are the ones who have managed to escape the big guns so long that it is apparent that they are better at ducking than you could ever be at hitting. The best variety of this species is Self-Sufficient Sam, who keeps an immaculate house, prepares excellent meals, shops with skill, and declines your offer to sew on a button (because he could do it better). If he is past forty and has begun to refer to himself as "confirmed," what we might say "set in his ways," so much the better.

Gorgeous George: GG's compulsion to strike poses never abates, and he has never been caught in an unflattering one. Those questioning him on the subject are advised (by him) that the reason is, quite simply, he has no bad angles. If you fall helplessly in love with him (his angles are pretty good), he will understand perfectly and welcome you to the club—of which he is self-appointed lifetime president.

Penny-Pincher Paul: PPP still has the first dollar he ever made. You will be able to spot Paul when you observe him studying a restaurant bill for fifteen minutes and questioning the waiter about several items on it before finally deciding to pay (after giving the waiter a fifty-cent tip on an eight-dollar lunch). And since he claims never to have small bills (nor does he want to spend the large ones), he is usually big on subways and buses. Or he may suggest a play for which "twofers" are available, although neither of you has any real interest in it.

If you have been accused of being extravagant and plan to stop working when you get married, this specimen should be your prime target.

T. Symington Snob: To the purple born, T. Symington speaks about his ancestors' voyage over on the *Mayflower* the way some of us talk about our cousin's subway trip to Flatbush. And when he speaks of equality for the masses, he means the equal opportunity and privilege for them to serve their "betters."

Never to be seen dead or alive at any but *the* most exclusive gathering places at *the* most prestigious table, T. Symington has preferences so select that only three waiters, the owner, and he know of their existence. Not unexpectedly, the delicacies he commands are all out of season, imported from someplace no one has ever heard of (where he also vacations) or, in the case of wine, from the year of the grape catastrophe when only two bottles were corked.

Obviously, if you could land T. Symington it would be a large *plume* in your *chapeau,* so the next time he looks down his nose at you, smile back engagingly. And try to convince yourself that he can be humanized and brought down to earth with a little of your everyday, loving, common touch.

Willie Weirdo: Willie has been considered slightly eccentric ever since he was four and fell into a waterhole while admiring himself, back in his home town of Kokomo. But the small-town squares never really, like, dug where he was coming from so he quit the scene in search of bigger waterholes. He digs the big city because he can lose his identity and let it all hang out there. (Nothing like back home, where even the town hermit knew all the gossip, from cradle to grave.) Willie is six-foot-plus and could be a dream if only he knew what a comb was for and weren't convinced that the more tattered your jeans and clothes are, the "funkier," "kinkier," and "hipper" people will think you are. His favorite outfit is a pair of ragged sneakers featuring the toe-out effect on one shoe, with torn jeans adorned with a rising sun in the middle of the derrière, a "sweat" shirt (the word is used advisedly) with an obscenity on the back, a band around his head, a large handkerchief hanging from one back pocket (just to the right of the sun). At times he adds a spotted calf vest— grease-spotted—for "dress up" occasions.

If you work for a staid company, say in their executive development program, and know the company is very big on protocol and decorum, Willie might be well worth considering.

Orson Too Old: If you are of a mind that you would rather be an old man's darling than a young man's fool, you might try Orson. True, everyone says he's too old for you, but he is young at heart—though hardly in anything else. The reason the big "O" likes you is that he thinks young girls can help him recapture his youth. He drools unashamedly over every sweet young thing who comes within grasp of his hot, albeit gnarled, hands. You can, however, take heart in the fact that he swears he likes you best, has a comfortable income, a small boat, and a house on the Cape that he has named "The Innocents." If you settle on this one, think of the pure pain-pleasure you can enjoy when the old coot abandons you for someone even younger.

Manny Mobster: Manny always has oodles of cash on hand even though he has no visible means of support. Sometimes known as Cigar Manny, Big Man Manny, or Manny the Man, he is always great fun to go out with because he is obviously powerful and gets star treatment at the clubs around town. Besides, he is very generous, often giving you fabulous gifts (the only favor he is likely to ask is that you keep a small package for him for a few days, or perhaps deliver it to a friend of his). He may even treat you to a luxurious trip to Europe, his only request being that you pick up a suitcase from a designated location and bring it back home, Doll. Or he may ask you to cash a large check for a friend of his in the hospital.

Manny may have a record, but if so it was a case of mistaken identity, or a frame-up. When you learn that his father used to beat his mother, him, and all his little brothers and sisters every Saturday night, and that if he hadn't stolen milk at six in the morning the family would have gone hungry, tears will come to your eyes (*sweet* Manny!), especially when you hear how he never got any Christmas gifts and always had to wear patched clothes to school—until he quit at age ten.

If you manage to become seriously involved with Manny, even if he treats you well there is always the distinct possibility that the police may prove less considerate if, as is likely, some of your dealings for the big "M" cause you to run afoul of the law. And, certainly, a turn in prison might be just what some punishment-seeking potential molls are hankering for.

Marryin' Dan: If he has already been married more than three times he is clearly a fine wrong-man possibility because, although he is obviously the marrying kind, the odds are you will finally be rejected just like your predecessors. Or he might prove so impossible to live with (that is, compatible with your neurosis) that you could end up in a long-term relationship, obviously rich in rejection potential.

The Clutterers

You have already seen how you can select unlikely or improbable types by pretending to think they are likely or probable, or because you convince yourself you can change them. However, there are some types so impossible in character, habits, or dress, not to mention all three, that no one, not even the girl most oriented toward hopeless projects, could mistake them or convert them. (Examples: The carelessly attired overweight Mr. Happy-Go-Lucky, who shows up to take you to an exclusive club in a plaid fingertip hunting jacket he can't button over his paunch. Or the big-spender sport from uptown who regales a group with a barrage of embarrassing jokes and otherwise holds forth all night but becomes thunderingly silent and lapses into acute amnesia, complicated by incipient paralysis, when he must locate his wallet at bill-paying time.)

These types, which I call "clutterers," are so low on the social totem pole that not only would you find them personally unacceptable, you wouldn't even pass them off on an unsuspecting out-of-town visitor. Despite all this, they can still serve a useful function in your scheme for rejection fulfillment. On the loose theory that one day they may be able to provide some undefined service—or even a service you would be well advised to get elsewhere—encourage them just enough to keep them hanging on as clutterers.

Certain philosophies have been found especially effective in helping one accumulate clutterers. One of the best is: Let pity rule your heart (i.e., the more woebegone, downtrodden, or hopeless the prospect, the more inclined you should be to freely give out your phone number, address, etc.). Another beaut: Having someone around, no matter how impossible, is better than having no one. Finally, all neurotics, like celebrities, need "blockers" to guard them, presumably from the bad but actually from the good.

You will find that collecting clutterers requires little real effort. In fact, in the absence of any conscious resolve to keep your life free of them, you will find that they seem to accumulate almost as a matter of course.

To derive maximum benefit from clutterers' presence, you should know something about the various categories.

The Good Joe Clutterer

This type usually works in your office building, lives in the neighborhood, or frequents some place you do, and only through a quirk of fate does a nodding relationship develop between you.

He is the antithesis of everything you had in mind about a man. Most often he is shorter than you, possesses a terrible sense of clothes, wears odd glasses unattractively perched on his nose, and usually is a man of few (and uninteresting) words. But one day you accept his timely offer—a favor of some kind, such as a lift in a driving rain, an assist with heavy groceries, etc. When it develops that he can repair your TV and is available to chauffeur you around or perform similar chores, you begin availing yourself of his services. Before long, Good but Unlikely Joe has insinuated himself into the scheme of things, as a sort of flunky dash admirer, and general clutterer.

While there is no suggestion of romance and you are just friends, it is, of course, tacitly understood that he has a crush on you. Considering this, and the fact that you are too clever to pay him for his services from the start, the least you can do is allow him the occasional opportunity to catch his breath over a cup of coffee and a sandwich, while enjoying the pleasure of your company and sneaking admiring glances.

It can be on one of these occasions that someone you have been dying to hear from phones, saying he is in the neighborhood and was thinking of dropping by, or has just fallen heir to a couple of theater tickets to a prize-winning play, or has suddenly learned of a great party and would like to pick you up shortly. Since common courtesy decrees that you not abruptly push the clutterer aside just after he has performed some uncompensated chore, you are effectively cluttered.

Or the Good Joe may drop by wearing his shirttail out, or with his grimy canvas hat turned up all around and sitting at a jaunty angle on the back of his head, to see if there is anything you need. If this visit coincides with one by a very distinguished prospect who had just been complimenting you on your discriminating taste, the effect can be devastating—if not downright conclusive.

The Inherited Clutterer

When a dear girl friend who is herself in the rat race of social life and looking for a target to call her own magnanimously offers one of her discoveries to you as "someone you will surely adore," it will usually turn out that she is house-cleaning clutterers and throwing one your way.

Accept her selfless offer. Be as charming as you can with her friend. (After all, you would not want him to report back that you were uninteresting, or less desirable than she.)

You may have to grit your teeth and bear the boredom during the evening out with your new acquisition, but your reward will be forthcoming. Numerous subsequent phone calls for dates, some of which may be difficult to refuse gracefully—and another clutterer for the collection.

The Ol' Reliable Clutterer

This type has been on the scene for some time—always there when you need him and too often when you don't.

He is sufficiently presentable for all occasions, and you date him on what must be described as a steady basis. The only slight complication arises from the fact that you date him only because there is no one else available, and you are constantly hoping to meet someone new. But Ol' Reliable hovers over you like a mother hen whenever you are out together. Moreover, he is romantically attracted to you, though you secretly detest his kisses and are annoyed by his caresses.

By all means, continue this "convenient" arrangement, although it is obvious that there is no tolerable future with him. After all, you can depend on him to lessen your chances of being free to develop any possible new find, and he will keep you in an unpleasant mood while you search.

The Telephone Clutterer

The telephone clutterer, with little to say and hardly any encouragement from you to say it, is nonetheless able to tie up your phone for ridiculous periods, often keeping more important calls from getting through. With just a little cooperation from you—after all, you don't want to be rude—he can tie up the line for hours.

Another function of this specialist is to interrupt you just as you are trying to get dressed for a big date. His calls usually occur when you are already running late. It would appear that some of the more expert technicians in the field work with a built-in divining rod that enables them to detect running water being drawn for the bath. After having allowed you sufficient time to get into the tub and soaped, they tend to dial your number. Or, when really perverse, drop in unannounced.

The Wonderful Clutterer

Although it may seem a contradiction in terms, the wonderful clutterer really does exist. He could, for instance, be an old flame for whom you continue to carry a faintly flickering torch. Since you still find him attractive, and thrive on the drawn-out rejection he provides, you allow him certain privileges of dropping by unexpectedly after weeks of absence to say hello, use the phone without permission, get a beer from the fridge, talk about "Mom" (yours, not his), and otherwise absorb oxygen which a new prospect (who may be present) could better use. (If you are alone, it may be understood that he can sleep with you on demand.)

And, too, this group also includes any other of the "wonderful ones" you realize that you can never have, yet afford priority position to, so that they can interfere with more promising discoveries.

What to Do If the Right Man Gets Snared, or the Challenge of Unexpected Success

Although it doesn't happen often, there are occasions when a girl's determination to choose the wrong man is dealt a severe blow by some unexpected twist of fate. (This shattering experience might be compared to the jolt one receives when trying to take another step down on a staircase when one has already taken the last step—multiplied a hundredfold.)

In this situation, a girl, in spite of having carefully avoided snaring a really desirable man (as outlined in these pages) (confident that he can never be won anyway), actually *gets* the man.

When we consider that, very often, this "impossible" prospect has been idolized, revered, and at times relentlessly pursued—all with the inner confidence that he was unattainable (safely married, completely out of her range or category, or whatever)—we can see the rude shock this could have on a girl's nervous system. Clearly, this problem calls for draconian tactics.

Whereas the rose-colored glasses through which you doubtless observed your target when you thought he could never be yours only highlighted his best features, a more critical appraisal is now in order, to illuminate previously unnoticed nooks and crannies.

Almost inevitably, to most people's surprise (not the least of whom is the formerly revered target), many faults and flaws now become visible. Former assets can now be looked on with contempt. For example, although you may have once admired him because of his ambition, his dedication to his job, and the fact that his boss relies so heavily on him, you can now complain that he is married to his job and mentally classify him as a kind of boot licker. Even if you were once proud of his junior executive title, bear in mind that he has held it for several years now and he appears to be going nowhere fast. While you may once have marveled from afar at his beautifully tailored clothes, impressive car, and ability to take frequent trips abroad, you should now be able to see everything quite differently. Actually, he is superficial, selfish, and vain, unwilling to spend money on anyone or anything but himself, concerned only with his own person and trappings.

Begin to pay more attention to his mannerisms; with a little effort you can convert them to manias. Note how he always squashes out his cigarettes in the remains of his dinner plate (which he invariably chooses over the ashtray nearby). Or how, whenever he's trying to make a big impression, he readjusts his tie and juts out his chin. Note too his way of completing sentences for people, or gratuitously supplying improved adjectives that make their thoughts more explicit.

Not only will you be much less impressed by and interested in him, but your changed attitude will generally cause him to become less interested in you.

Remember, then: In these extreme and unexpected cases, don't panic. You can quickly and easily convert the positive to the negative. In fact, the more positive the original features, the more negative potential available. Consider, for example, the following JK chart.

The formula is: two positive Before Available (B.A.) equals double negative After Available (A.A.):

B.A.	A.A.
Persevering	Inflexible
Tactful	Hypocritical
Discriminating	Snobbish
Sentimental	Mushy
Ambitious	Pushy
Poised	Conceited
Intelligent	Pedantic
Easygoing	Apathetic
Protective	Possessive
Generous	Extravagant
Well-organized	Fussy
Spontaneous	Impetuous
Unaffected	Unpolished
Avant-garde	An oddball
Sensuous	Lascivious
Congenial	Spineless
Resolute	Stubborn
Discreet	Sneaky
Sophisticated	Phony
Affectionate	Sloppy
Aggressive	Overbearing
Contained	Stiff
Alert	A show-off
Carefree	Nonproductive
Concerned	Interfering
Free-hearted	A sucker
Methodical	Old-maidish
Responsive	Rash
Down-to-earth	Countrified
Original	Weird
Passionate	Oversexed
Agreeable	Unmanly

How to Play the Late Game

The advantages that this technique offers are apparent, since it is a favorite exercise not only of successful failures in matters of the heart but in every other conceivable field. If you are failure-oriented, you probably already engage in some aspects of it, but for best results you should learn the fine points that can turn amateur into pro overnight.

The object, of course, is to see how long you can keep a prospect waiting beyond the appointed hour. It is a technique both effective in itself and when used in conjunction with other techniques. Surprisingly enough, good timing is one of the most important factors to consider. If you arrive too late, your date may be gone; if you are not late enough, no damage will have been done.

For beginners at the game, a late arrival of only thirty-five or forty minutes is recommended. This is based on the theory that anyone interested enough to ask you out would wait patiently at least fifteen or twenty minutes. If you have not arrived at the end of that time, the target will usually allow you "just fifteen minutes more," vowing to leave if you don't appear by then. When you still fail to show, several more minutes of grace are usually won.

Until you get the feel of the game you must content yourself with this limited and admittedly not altogether fulfilling goal. However, before long you should be able to keep him waiting twice as long, ever bearing in mind that the final objective is to wear his patience so thin it is almost (but not quite) at the breaking point. Then he will have little forbearance left to deal with the other capers you will perform.

When setting the time for the encounter, leave it as flexible as possible. Ask, "Shall we say between eight and eight-thirty?" You will find few men so unchivalrous as to leave at eight-thirty, when you have just begun to be late (although by one criterion you have already kept him waiting half an hour). If he is someplace where he can be reached by phone, call him fifteen or twenty minutes after the latest time mentioned and promise to be there in ten minutes. This is good for at least another half hour.

The pre-late-arrival explanation, to prepare him for the worst and give his patience food for survival, can be another helpful delaying tactic. Tell him how in spite of your efforts and firm resolve you have great difficulty *ever* being on time. Then, encourage him by your assurance that he can count on your dependability and ultimate presence. Another way to prepare him for your late arrival is by explaining that you may be delayed because of working overtime, having to wait for a delivery, or having to stop somewhere. When you are half an hour late, he may call you to see what happened. Tell him you were, as predicted, detained, but you will be there forthwith—and so you will, one hour later.

The Impatient Types

Some men are difficult to keep waiting, even by the most expert late-game player. For these forty-five-minutes-tops types, special preparations are needed to add the dimension of confusion and anxiety to the waiting, so that three-quarters of an hour has the same disgust value as an hour and a half for less impatient men.

For these types, submerge all details in confusion by changing the time, place, and even day several times, leaving him uncertain if you, or even he, finally understood the basic details. Select a meeting place where there are several entrances. When you do not arrive in a reasonable time at one entrance, he will be forced to dash back and forth to see if you are at another one.

Meetings in trains and bus stations are also high on the list of recommended sites, not only because the waiting time seems twice as long (since you are expected to arrive on each incoming train or bus), but also because he must keep busy checking the crowd to make sure he doesn't lose you.

Other recommended places are street corners near banks or loan offices, where his waiting could arouse suspicion, and areas of a public park where there are no benches. If he has a car, anyplace rife with No Parking signs, so that he will be forced to go around in circles while waiting, is fine.

The least appropriate place is a restaurant or bar where he can be seated and comfortable, although he may feel rather foolish waiting for you for a full hour after he has told the waiter you will be arriving shortly and he will not order until then.

The Excuse

Preparing a good excuse is an integral part of any late-game planning. Some of the time-tested are:

1. The tried and true clichés: (a) You were confused about the time agreed upon (naturally always under the impression that it was later). (b) Your watch was slow. (c) You took a nap and your alarm clock didn't work. (d) You got caught in crosstown (downtown, midtown, highway) traffic. (e) As you were pressing the dress you planned to wear, you scorched it (broke the zipper, stained it, tore it, or otherwise eliminated it) and had to find something else to wear. (f) You couldn't get a taxi (if you came by train, one pulled out just as you were walking into the station). (g) You broke the heel of your shoe and had to go back upstairs for another pair. (h) The cleaners did not deliver the suit you had planned to wear.

2. Excuses that show how inconsiderate you are, or telegraph other unattractive personality traits: (a) You were in the midst of an exciting novel or TV show and wanted to find out how it ended. (b) You became so involved in the biannual shoe sale at your favorite department store that the time simply got away from you. (c) You received a

phone call as you were about to leave and didn't want to appear rude. (d) You were delayed at the beauty shop trying a new facial a friend had recommended. (e) You took your pet cat to the veterinarian to leave it for shots, but decided to wait for it after its fur began to rise, poor thing. (f) Your boss worked late, and you remained until just after he left to impress him with the depth of your dedication. (g) You ran into a friend and must have talked with him longer than you realized (or, better yet, he prevailed on you to have a drink).

3. Farfetched, way-out excuses: (a) You had left home and almost reached the place where you were supposed to meet him when you remembered you had left the iron or the oven on; or not closed the window (rain was threatening); or not closed the fire-escape window (there have been a rash of burglaries in your building). (b) You were lost in thoughts and missed your stop on the train. (c) You were out of the house, the door had locked behind you, and you realized you didn't have your keys. You couldn't locate the super and had to climb across the terrace of your next-door neighbor and shimmy up the fire escape. (d) You were all dressed and ready to leave when someone came from building maintenance with an electrician (plumber, fire inspector, or other appropriate functionary) to try to locate a potentially dangerous electrical short. (e) A friend of yours came by unexpectedly and was depressed (or, if you're feeling dramatic, was contemplating suicide), and you did not have the heart to tell her that you were going out. Since you didn't want to bring her along, you had to sit and chat with her until she finally decided to leave.

4. Choice, blue-chip excuses: (a) You developed a slight headache and had decided not to come until you realized you'd have to come out anyway to have dinner, go to the cleaners, or perform some other minor chore. (b) You had forgotten that this was indeed the evening of your date with him, until something happened to remind you at the last minute.

When He Picks You Up at Home

Since even girls with good intentions, for reasons best known to psychiatrists, often employ late-game tactics, most men have had unpleasant exposure to them. As a result, many men may insist on picking you up at home. With a little imagination on your part, however, you can play the game just as effectively in the setting of his choice.

You have doubtless noticed that it is always easier to do something you have been putting off for months when you are supposed to be doing something else. (Is that clear?) Therefore, the night of a big date would be the best time to begin that long-threatened self-improvement program. If it is posture, practice improving it before the mirror; if it is better diction, read your favorite poetry aloud, enunciating clearly and carefully for half an hour or so. To wake up lifeless hair, bend over to improve the circulation and brush with two brushes about one hundred strokes. Invigorate your skin with a steam facial, followed by a cold-water rinse and the luxurious application of your favorite cream.

Improve your surroundings, too. Clean out the catch-all hall closet, discarding everything you have not worn for three seasons. Examine all your shoes, leaving out those that need recapping. Check your dresser drawers. If they are something less than tidy, with loose earrings, necklaces tangled with thread and ribbons, tape measures and stray stockings, empty the contents onto the bed so as to assort, fold, and rearrange everything. By now, your date should be arriving. Hurriedly try to establish some semblance of order, throwing everything back into the drawers, gathering up the shoes and old clothes and tissuing off the creamy evidence of your self-improvement program. As your date waits by the door, hearing the hustle and bustle within, it will be almost as uncomfortable and suspenseful as not knowing whether he is waiting at the right entrance. When you finally go to the door, put him at his ease immediately by asking him why he has come early (even if he's late). Apologize for the house and your appearance and promise to be ready in fifteen minutes flat. Then go to the bathroom and start your bath.

Since he thoughtlessly arrived before you were ready, you will naturally feel tense. Be a bit testy with him; it will make you feel better. Further relax during your bath, when you should make two important decisions: first, realize that no matter how you rush now you cannot possibly be ready on time; second, since you are already late and he must wait until you are ready, you should try to look so smashing he will feel his waiting was worth while.

After your bath, apply makeup meticulously. Recall several articles you have read about ways to apply rouge to highlight your eyes, and change the contours of your face, making it more interesting. Experiment with other beauty tips you have seen. Wash your face and start again when you are not satisfied with the results.

It is a foregone conclusion that your hair, which has a mind of its own, will never cooperate and fall right when you most want it to. If it doesn't respond when you comb it carefully, comb it indifferently, as you do when you are about to put curlers in it for bed. After all, it often looks best at that time.

If a phone call interrupts your primping and it is one of your girl friends, it might be a good idea to ask her which of two or three outfits you are considering would be best in her opinion. Then, of course, you may have to listen to why she called you. If the caller is a man, you will not want to dismiss him too abruptly. Even if he is someone completely impossible, give him enough encouragement to keep him calling at times like these and to generally interfere with your relationship with someone who could be important to you.

When you pick an ensemble, do not do so without careful consideration. Consider your girl friend's choice, but do not forget that girls are often jealous and the one she recommended could just be the least flattering of the lot. For fun, try it on and look at it critically to see if she's sincere.

An hour to an hour and a half later, when you enter your living room, always have a clever remark prepared relative to how times flies. Say, "How tempus fugits, eh?" or something equally witty. After you finally declare yourself ready, suddenly remember something you have to start looking for: keys, a glove, a magazine with unusual restaurant suggestions—but only after he has stood up, put on his hat and coat, and given every indication that he is prepared to leave.

If you happen to be the type who is compulsively punctual, the gymnastics involved in playing the late game may be as disconcerting to you as to the man in question, and other methods must be considered.

Giving Him the Gold Rush

> *"A girl who makes it obvious she weighs men in karats instead of pounds, and has nothing on her mind behind the dollar signs in her eyes, may attract some successful prospectors temporarily. But, when it comes to someone wanting to stake a permanent claim, she will usually wind up as popular as a ghost town."*
>
> —*J. K.*

Although my observations and research have led me to formulate the above philosophy, it is good to also introduce a dissenting voice in order to put the matter into proper perspective. One of the most articulate of these is Linda-Marvine R. A tall, stunning—if slightly over-adorned—redhead from the deep South, Linda-Marvine described herself as a trained laboratory technician when we met in the laundry room some three years ago. Since I never heard her mention a job, I gathered that her "laboratory" was her apartment; that she was a "trained technician" there seemed little doubt. Indeed, as she began to take me into her confidence and tell me of some of her "experiments," I was duly impressed. Last year there was the multimillionaire real-estate tycoon who pursued her like hot property for three or four months, took her off to Aruba, and bought her a fourth fur coat before losing interest and leaving her like an abandoned building. And then there was the Wall Street broker who recognized her assets for a time and guided her in some wise investments before turning from bullish to bearish on her.

However, when I mentioned one day to her that I considered gold-digging techniques among the best counterproductive methods for alienating men, she was quick to offer her assessment. "Hell," she said, "the sons of bitches are going to leave you even if you give *them* money. So the best thing to do is follow the Boy Scouts' motto and always be prepared—getting as much as you can while you can." She reminded me how "Sonny-the-rat," her boy friend of yore, an unemployed actor whom she supported for several years, starred in a vanishing act as soon as he landed his first TV commercial. "Use men or be used," she warned. Then, warming to her subject, "What about a married man?" she asked rhetorically. "Doesn't he have to maintain or 'pay' his wife if he wants to sleep with her? And if he doesn't, can't she have him put out?" And then she reminded me of the well-known story of Lady X, high-born, proud but poor, who was offered a small fortune to share her favors with a certain gentleman. When finally she consented, the lady heard the sum reduced to near zero. To which she asked, in a huff, "What do you think I am?" "That, madam," he replied, "has already been established. The only question now is price."

"Everyone has a price," said my friend, "even if it's marriage."

My own position is that while I have nothing against gold digging per se—on the contrary—I only contend that most men smart enough to earn a lot of money are smart enough to know most of the games women will play to try to make them part with it. And sooner or later be alienated by the conniving. But since, in the final analysis, this is doubtless what you really want, dig while the digging's good.

Formulating a Strong Basic Credo

As you go prospecting for gold, always take with you a strong basic credo. Not only will it enable you to brush aside anyone who cannot meet your financial expectations, it can also be counted on to turn off those who can—as you reveal how crass you really are.

You have already seen some of the "gems" on which Linda-Marvine bases her credo. Below are several others you may find useful:

1. A man values something more if he has to pay for it.

2. A girl has to protect her own interests because a man cannot be counted on to do it for her.

3. If a man wants a woman to satisfy his demands, he should be prepared to satisfy hers.

4. If a man wants a car, a trip abroad, or anything else, he is prepared to pay for it. So . . .

5. A man who really cares about a woman should be pleased to make her happy by giving her things she wants.

6. A man may tell a woman anything, but dollars speak louder than words.

7. In this society, where money is power, it is how much you have that counts, not how you got it.

8. Money (or gifts left behind) can help compensate you for the rejection that you can inevitably expect (have no illusions that an affair might endure).

9. Love may be fine for Juliet (look where it got her), but remember: diamonds are a girl's best friend.

10. So is money.

Sifting for Gold Dust

Sifters might be defined as petty gold diggers. They usually alienate men early on in the game with petty, transparent attempts to "take" them for whatever relatively insignificant amount they can through various subtle devices. Here are some of the best known:

1. Ask your target to go shopping with you at a market or drug store and act as if you are deaf, paralyzed, or do not understand English when the clerk announces the amount you owe.

2. Just happen to be looking through a desk full of bills the first time he comes to visit you. No matter what subject he discusses, do not let your conversation stray from your petty debts and the money you need to pay them.

3. If he is sending you home in a cab, tell him the fare is three times what it really is (if he calls the next day, "forget" and tell him about something that happened on the subway on your way home).

4. When en route home after a late night on the town with someone who appears to be quite smitten with you, begin to talk about how exhausted you are and how much you would love to take the next day off if only you could afford it.

5. If someone gives you a gift, sweetly protest that he shouldn't have, then ask him if he still has the receipt, explaining that you plan to return it for the money.

Hunting for Nuggets

If you have a bigger ante in mind, you will need a bit more effort and patience. For, unless you are a professional, a play-for-pay type, you will have to convince your target that you like him for himself, not for his money. Well-heeled men know full well what an asset their wealth represents, and even advertise it in various displays of conspicuous consumption. But generally they are outraged at the thought that some woman may be after them only for their money.

In order to inspire confidence in him, continually profess to be in awe of the workings of his mind—the precision and logic, the sparkling wit, the unbelievable imagination—and his body—his sexual prowess (it is so different with him, so exciting and new, as if he had invented an entirely new art form). Compliment him on his impeccable taste in dressing. Make your schedule flexible to accommodate his, never bitching if he has to break a date. Pretend to economize for him by complaining about items on a restaurant menu that are excessively priced, ordering the more moderately priced ones to convince him of your sincerity.

When he seems to be duly impressed, but you are still in the dark as to how much you can safely put the bite on him for, begin a "discreet" inquiry among his friends and acquaintances to establish his real worth. Or slyly question him to ascertain these same facts.

Then begin alluding repeatedly to your financial troubles. (This is the most offensive thing you can do, since he probably caught the hint the first time, and if there was no favorable response, it was doubtless because he was unwilling to offer assistance; repeating the hints is more apt to win you contempt than cold cash.)

When it becomes apparent that his interest in you is beginning to wane, think about all the time you have wasted with him, remembering that you have given him not only yourself but the equivalent of millions in flattery and undeserved compliments. Consider how unworthy he is: not bright at all, a dodo really. (He couldn't have made a penny if his father hadn't thoughtfully died and left him his money; he majored in getting kicked out of schools, you have learned, etc.) His taste? Early nouveau riche. Sex? Admit he's a lousy lay—you'd only been deceiving yourself because you had diamonds in your eyes.

Now that you are in the right frame of mind, decide that the next time you see the bastard you are going to make the "touch" no matter what. (Setting an inflexible schedule to make monetary requests is a must in any gold digger's plans.)

When you make the request, the more complicated the accompanying story, the better (which will improve the possibilities of ferreting out inconsistencies in it when you forget some key detail). For instance, tell him that you were ill last year, and spent a month in the hospital (be vague as to why). Say, "I've been paying them off but now they've threatened to garnishee my salary unless I pay the $981.44 balance *this week!*" Explain that you are up for a big promotion, and that this will surely kill your chances —in fact, if it happens, you might even lose your job. Tell him how you hate to ask him but are desperate and would really appreciate it if he could help you out. Begin to talk about how you could pay him back a little at a time . . . but let your voice trail off before making any firm commitment.

Don't have any contingency plans for the possibility that he may ask the name of the hospital so that he can have his lawyer intervene on your behalf, or even write a check to the place.

When it turns out that his assets—like his heart—are frozen, or he tells you he will see what he can do—which is usually nothing—bristle with barely concealed indignation. With no good reason now to conceal your contempt, you can treat him as he deserves to be treated, thus guaranteeing the final rejection you have been postponing in the hope you might extract a nugget or two from the guy.

Of course, if he really does like you and is as trusting and sympathetic as he is generous, he may agree to help you with the needed dollars. If he does, instead of appreciating his gesture, think how gullible he is, and how stupid, and try to conceive of another ruse to get more money out of him. Remember, if at first you don't succeed in alienating a target, try, try again.

Repressing the Delicate Condition

We have all seen movies and read novels depicting the much-sought-after, violet-scented heroine in days of yore who spent most of her time daintily fanning, delicately coughing, or being revived from fainting spells with the aid of the smelling salts she always carried in her ruffled sleeves.

In the twentieth century, such heroines are known as duds. Today's man wants a woman who can share his fun and activities at a party, on the tennis court, the ski slopes, beach, or wherever. A girl who is too delicate to do anything but throw a wet blanket over the festivities will naturally be scrupulously avoided.

If you are the delicate, fragile type, by all means feature it wherever you go, and overemphasize it in whatever you do. Although some men prefer a woman who is basically dependent on him, precious few would want one who seems destined to develop into a basket case in the first few years of a relationship.

Remember to make full use of special situations. For instance, on any outing with him, try to be completely incompatible with and unable to tolerate the environment. If you are skiing together, find the glare of the sun on the snow blinding. If he offers you anti-glare goggles, complain that they irritate your tender skin. Be unable to tolerate the cold because your hands were once frostbitten. If you decide to ski, remind him that you must be careful because your bones are small and fragile. Ski at a snail's pace and demand he stay close to you (especially if he's a crack skier).

At the beach, wear a tremendous hat to protect your delicate complexion from the sun or demand a chair with an umbrella. Explain that you must have proper facilities to change into your bathing suit (which would be ruined if it got wet). After the first half hour, complain about the heat and sand and insist that you be taken home. Appear to be continuously ailing, or intricately involved in some special, arcane formula to prevent you from ailing. On a scorching day, insist that the car be hermetically sealed to protect allergy-sensitive areas from road dust, pollen, etc. Needless to say, smoking is prohibited. (If ever you spot a target who is an obvious chain smoker, this technique can drive him mad in no time flat.)

Make a big issue about the necessity of getting meals at a fixed, nonnegotiable hour, and of rigidly conforming to the nightly retirement patterns you have established for yourself. Even if you are someplace where no restaurants are immediately available, or in the midst of some extraordinary event or celebration, explain that you cannot safely vary from your routine. After all, your health is at stake.

If ever you decide to risk life and limb to engage in sexual relations with someone, you can and should apply the same technique. Claim to be "built small," even if it is evident that you are not. Tell him that it is the first time—or practically—for you, even though you have been making this claim for several years.

Remain tense throughout the experience, apprehensive of some potential pain or damage to your delicate person. If there is the slightest incompatibility in size, as you sense your partner's excitement reaching a peak, burst into tears and ask him to please stop.

Your justification for being and playing delicate is that it makes you seem more feminine and therefore makes a man feel more powerful and masculine. For once, he has a woman who does not represent the usual challenge to him. However, though some men may appreciate this notion, at least to a degree, if you prove too delicately feminine to indulge in the fundamental act generally considered vital to the flowering of male-female relations, you can count on early rejection fulfillment. (For further horizontal details, see Part III.)

The "I'm Not That Kind of Girl" Charade

Though you are *not* "that kind of girl," dress and do everything possible to convey the impression that you are.

When the man you have openly enticed, deliberately provoked, and visually seduced all evening learns at the moment of truth that you are *not* that kind of a girl, the relationship is unlikely to survive the shock.

As for dress, obviously you should wear as often as possible the low-on-top-high-at-bottom ones, those that are on a clinging, bias cut, and the second-skin knit variety.

Your hair should be worn free and swinging, to parallel the moral attitude you want to convey; and, bearing in mind that good legs, like great talent, should be exhibited, remember to hoist your skirt when you sit down.

When he comes to pick you up for the evening (the event cannot be staged anyplace where total surrender is possible), let your glance meet his (seductively) when his survey of the "booty" finally ascends to your eyes. Your smile should be sensuous and dreamy.

If you dance, let it be close; and should your moist lips accidentally brush his cheek, so much the better.

As the evening progresses, pretend to drink too much. By all means refrain from doing so, but start to bubble and fizz like champagne anyway. Sit on his lap; giggle at off-color stories; if the music so inspires you, offer your solo rendition of the best bumps of burlesque and throw in a few of your own grinds for good measure. Toss off your shoes with great abandon, expressing a need to be close to nature.

At hand-holding time, give him squeeze for squeeze, as if to confirm some secret agreement. Sizzle along at this torrid temperature, only stopping short of a verbal commitment (which he is unlikely to demand with such an obvious understanding). Only when the palpitating alienation target moves in for the kill do you begin to show signs that you are not familiar with the rules of the game. Say, "Your house? Why should I go to your house?" Or, "What do you mean, some place we can be alone?" "Relax? But I'm already relaxed." When he is finally forced to reveal the name of the game, wax indignant, explaining that you are *not* that kind of girl. Then flounce away, the picture of injured virtue.

If he graciously insists on escorting you home in a desperate effort to touch your heart with his gallantry and perhaps have the opportunity to get you into a more conducive atmosphere, relent and consent. Kiss and giggle in the taxi. After you arrive at your door, however, explain that he cannot come in because your roommate is sleeping on the couch, your mother is arriving in town in the morning, and your landlord does not allow you to entertain men at late hours. After all, you are *not* that kind of a girl!

Do not, however, make the mistake of asking him, "What kind of girl do you think I am?" He may just tell you.

The Argument Arsenal

Some girls are reluctant to use their physical attributes in their alienation campaign against men. If this is the case with you, I recommend the Argument Arsenal.

Weapons from this stockpile are indispensable to a girl in her struggle to project a negative image. Try to select at least one to be carried with you constantly, in a holster strapped just beneath the chip on your shoulder.

The valuable and popular weapons in this arsenal include the Debater, Trifle Rifle, Repeater, and the Personal Attacker. Their prestige and importance derive not only from their demonstrated effectiveness but also from their versatility and the ease with which they can be pressed into service. No previous preparations are required, no particular setting necessary. An audience, though at times helpful, is by no means essential. In addition, they are highly portable, and one or the other type often can, when employed at a first meeting with a likely prospect, result in almost immediate rejection fulfillment.

The Debater

This big gun from the arsenal can have two distinct effects, depending on which type of ammunition is loaded into it, type #1 or #2. Type #1 ammo is made up of statistics, research data, expert opinion, and solid-fuel information. When it is loaded into the debater by girls clever enough to handle it and sufficiently overbearing to discharge the full force, it "levels" the point of view of any interested male who dares challenge their insecure position by disagreeing with them. The desired side effect of such an assault is, of course, that incalculable damage is done to the male ego in question.

Type #2 ammo is for girls who do not choose or are not mentally equipped to make use of type #1 but want to profit from the destructive benefits of Debater attacks anyway. This mixture is composed of unsubstantiated "facts," arbitrary conclusions, and vigorous though uninformed assaults on the position of any man who tries to engage them in friendly conversation. When Debaters so loaded are fired, the effect is to becloud the issue rather than clarify it, ultimately add more heat than light to it, and smoke out the potential target.

For those girls who choose type #1: Convince yourself that the reason for your boning up on every subject under the sun is to be able to discuss them intelligently, since this should impress men. Take special interest in all controversial subjects and form inflexible, steadfast opinions on each (the more contradictory the prevailing expert opinion, the better).

Then, the next time you are with someone who seems to like you, casually introduce the most controversial subject you can think of.* Sometimes a consideration of the background of the man in question can suggest a proper choice. For example, if you know he is of old-line, conservative, Republican stock, begin a discussion of Watergate, or perhaps extol the accomplishments and virtues of a certain very liberal Democratic candidate or officeholder, especially praising any program he espouses that involves large sums of public money. Say, "I think the welfare budget should be switched with the military."

Or you may want to draw him into line of Debater fire by asking his opinion on a particular subject, pretending to want to know his views. After permitting him to express a (very) few of them, begin to challenge. Quote the latest statistics; ask questions that make him contradict himself or land him in a trap. If it develops that he is clearly incapable of defending his position in the face of your onslaught, try to find someone to observe the situation and watch him go down in defeat.

Reject any suggestions he may submit to "forget it" or "drop the subject"; refuse to settle for anything short of total, abject surrender.

When the adversary limps away from this battleground, it is very unlikely that your Saturday nights at home alone will be interrupted by a future call from him.

If you do not feel qualified to handle such explosive ammunition, try ammo #2. Remember, your lack of familiarity with a particular subject is by no means a handicap, since what you lack in knowledge you will make up in intensity and stubbornness.

---

* Anything pertaining to religion, politics, or sex is obviously particularly reliable. But remember: anything about which an opinion can be expressed can be turned into an argument.

In the absence of any informed views of your own, choose one of his that "just doesn't sound quite right" with which to take issue. Ask him how he can possibly hold such a ridiculous, immature, untenable, farfetched, absurd opinion. Your rebuttal should be prefaced by "everyone knows," "it has been proven," "as any fool should be able to see," etc. If he still remains unperturbed, interrupt him mid-sentence, accusing him of having interrupted *you*. If he offers you the opportunity to make your mark, simply continue firing your Debater indiscriminately at everything he has said.

Bear in mind that in using this technique you run the risk of having your prospect try to turn the tables on you. If this happens, don't panic: avoid answering any direct questions fired at you. Be especially cautious if he mentions apparently unrelated topics: he could be trying to change the subject and salvage whatever is left of the relationship.

If any of his apparent peace overtures begin to impress you, think of some injustice you have endured at the hands of one of the other members of his sex, who had also seemed *très sympathique* at first. And then load in more ammo.

If a third party can be involved, familiarize them with the discussion, carefully misrepresenting your opponent's position. If he disagrees with your interpretation, accuse him of being a turncoat. Say, "I can't believe my ears! Not ten minutes ago he was saying just the opposite!"

Somewhere in the course of discussions of this kind, it is always a good idea to refer to the fact that you subscribe to or frequently read the *Reader's Digest,* or other publications that will suggest the depth of your intellectualism.

Most men, after being subjected to such a Debater attack, will be more than eager to leave you all the free time you want to continue your reading and intellectual research.

The Trifle Rifle

Although one spray from this weapon is rarely lethal, the cumulative effects can be quite devastating. This one is recommended for use against your steady, since the pellets that lodge just beneath the skin do get on the nerves more and more as time goes by.

In cases where the Trifle Rifle is brought to bear, there is no obvious attack, only a subtle guerrilla offensive, with volleys of petty objections, complaints about minor infractions, and a great deal of whining, fretting, nagging, and prodding. Here are a few suggestions.

After a party where he has danced with other girls, complain and spray him for having neglected you. At the next party, when he stays by your side, accuse him of deliberately trying to stifle and inhibit you.

Find fault with the way he dresses. His hat is tilted to the side and looks silly. After he adjusts it, complain that he has plopped it on straight as if he were heading for a corn field. Or, when he comes over one evening to take you out, wearing his favorite suit:

YOU: Oh, you're wearing that suit tonight.

HE: Yeah. (*Pause.*) Why?

YOU: Nothing. I was just asking.

HE: But . . . You see I'm wearing it.

YOU: Yes. (*Pause.*)

HE: Don't you like this suit?

YOU: Well . . . actually . . . I don't like it very much.

HE: I thought it was one of my best suits. What's wrong with it?

YOU: (*pulling at the sleeve, lifting the tail of the jacket*): Oh, I don't know.

HE: Don't you like the color?

YOU: The color's okay, I guess.

HE: Well, what's wrong with it?

YOU: I don't know. I just . . . don't like it. It looks . . . funny. (*Pause.*) Maybe it just looks funny . . . on *you*.

Obviously, there is no redress for such an ambiguous, unspecific complaint.

Use your imagination and ingenuity to pick out various things to harp on, keeping up a steady spray. Remember, even though they may be minor, little things mean a lot, especially when they are under his skin.

The Repeater

This type of weapon is employed when your friend/lover has committed some appreciable offense, for which he has been roundly berated, exiled for a period of penitence, and allowed to return only after profuse apologies and, preferably, the gift of some irresistible trinket.

Normally, after the reconciliation, his original sin could be forgiven if not forgotten. But not so if you pack a repeater. In this case, every time he does something to annoy you, bring up all the details of this or some other supposedly dead issue, load your repeater with them, and discharge again.

For example, if he is late meeting you for the theater, shoot at him about the time he drank too much at the family reunion. Remind him how he insisted on talking to visiting Aunt Milly about the places he went to in Kansas City when he was a soldier, even though she kept trying to change the subject. Shoot every detail back into his face about how it was apparent to everyone in the room what type of places they were, how embarrassed you were, what your family said about him (word for word, of course), *ad nauseam*. It's simple—you'll know your lines better each time—and effective.

The Personal Attacker

Some women are not really content without the security of knowing they have an overkill capacity. For such thorough types, who wish to be able to relax in the knowledge that

144

not only the developing affair but any trace of simple friendly interest will be obliterated, the Personal Attacker is recommended.

Proficiency in the use of the Personal Attacker is not at all difficult. All that is required is the perception to define your victim's weakness(es) and the readiness to open fire.

Suggested targets range from any current rumor (obviously, foundation in fact is irrelevant), reflections on his masculinity (integrity, intelligence), derogatory remarks about his family (close friends, line of work), etc.

It is recommended that the Personal Attacker be resorted to only in the case of social emergencies or compulsive neurotic needs. This caution is suggested because a man can also be familiar with this weapon, and, though the devastation you wreak may be awesome, his retaliatory strike in the last throes could put you out of commission emotionally for some time.

How to Be a (Domestic) Pet Peeve

It is popularly assumed that excessive preoccupation of spinsters with cats, dogs, parrots, canaries, and the like is a result of their lonely existence. As a matter of fact, it can be reported on the basis of my own observations and a certain amount of solid hearsay evidence that this preoccupation with pets often precedes, and in fact contributes to, the maiden state.

Following are a group of attitudes and theories about domestic animals suggested for adoption by women who are not hoping to domesticate the higher forms of the species.

"Cats Are Cleaner Than People"

By simply accepting this premise and without actually making the statement as such, you will have made tremendous progress in alienating a number of men.

To support this attitude, point out the numerous ways in which cats demonstrate their dedication to cleanliness. Admire the daily top-to-bottom inclusive licking they give themselves with in-between touch-ups (lick-offs) when needed. Above all, remind skeptical parties how, after a trip to the kitty-litter box, the cat always cleans his little paws with his tongue.

Having been thus informed of kitty's devotion to personal hygiene, any interested male observer can understand why your cat is allowed certain liberties such as kitchen privileges with table-top rights and sink access, and permission to lounge on and stalk over sofa and overstuffed chairs among visitors, shedding as it goes.

If you decide to allow someone the rather questionable pleasure of watching you prepare dinner for him, with the cat acting as inspector on the scene, snooping and sniffing around the ingredients, gently remove the cat, but do not bother to wash your hands.

Make it a practice to feed the cat or dog from the table as you eat, so that when guests are present for dinner the little darling will come whining around the table in anticipation, licking the shoes, legs, and hands of the visitors. After dinner, place the dinner plate on the floor and allow kitty or doggy to lick it clean, as one would suspect it has often done before.

Do not make a secret of the warm and loving regard in which you hold kitty. Summon him to your loving arms. Nuzzle your nose into his spit-cleaned fur. Coo sweet nothings to him. Terminate this love scene with a shower of kisses. You will find that the more finicky chaps will rather pointedly avoid your subsequently offered embrace, not anxious to become a second-hand kitty kisser.

Will the Real Pet Please Stand Up?

In addition to showering your cat or other pet with affection, let the man in question begin to see that you are more concerned about it than him. Whenever he has planned something special, make some excuse about having to go home to feed (or walk) the animal. Or refuse to stay out late after work because it may become lonely for kitty back home.

Ask your date to go out and get food for your "baby" so he will be able to eat on schedule. This notwithstanding the fact that your target may be trying to watch an interesting television presentation or relax after a hard day. Or ask him to take the dog for a walk, handing him a big stick to take with him just in case the larger dogs that often attack your dog interfere.

"*Love Me, Love My Pet*"

Many a perfectly humane, God-fearing gentleman who is far from an advocate of cruelty to animals will nevertheless be utterly unreceptive to the idea of showing your pet certain considerations and deferences.

Tell him not to push kitty away when it licks his face. "That means he likes you. He doesn't do that to everybody." When kitty's claws get caught in his expensive tweed jacket, or when Fido jumps up on his light gabardine suit with his dirty paws, give him the same malarky.

When kitty comes sniffing or doggy comes growling around his chair, warn him not to ignore it, but to pick it up and make friends. Explain that the dog is there for your protection and won't harm him, but warn the gentleman that he should not play too rough with you or make any overly quick moves. Say jokingly, "Especially any moves toward *me*. The poor dear is insanely jealous!"

If he intimates that the beast makes him uncomfortable or in any way insinuates that you should get rid of it, decide that he is a person who does not like animals and cannot be trusted.

Expect him to rationalize away any allergies he may think he has to your cat, dog, bird, pet snake; etc. Show him that the sneezing, wheezing, red eyes, or runny nose is all his mind. Say, "If you want to go on seeing me, you'll have to learn to love Fido."

If you are able to secure a monkey for a pet, you will have made a real coup. When they are not busy scratching, digging, and making distracting noises, they often get into misunderstandings with visitors trying to be friendly and bite them.

Any time your monkey or any other pet bites one of your targets, chuckle and minimize the whole thing. Say, "It's his way of being affectionate." Better yet, act as if it were the victim's fault. Question him about what he did to your pet, accuse him of having gotten him excited, and mention how he's never bitten anyone else.

"Nothing's Too Good for My Baby"

Talk about how you purchase the best cuts of meat, select fish, and nothing but the finest of everything for your pet. Quote the high cost of such standards of excellence. This is especially advocated if you know that your prospect has only moderate means. Tell him how you allow your darling to sleep in your bed because you wouldn't dream of putting him in a hard old box.

Remember the general rules on pets. The negative benefits derived from having more than one increase geometrically. That is, two pets give the negative benefits of four, four of eight, etc. This is because they can chase each other about, fighting and playing, requiring far more attention than one. Also, two pets considerably increase the ever-present possibility that they will be smelled before they are seen.

Psychoanalyze It to Death

This technique is especially suited for women who have been, would like to be, or perhaps should be under analysis. Their preoccupation with the subconscious makes them particularly inclined to conclude that all answers and explanations are hidden somewhere therein, and to constantly probe beneath the surface of the simplest acts for involved, complex interpretations. With a bit of preparation and the right attitude and outlook, any basically adept female can soon master it.

As you approach your career as psychiatrist without portfolio, you must always remember that obvious conclusions should be discarded first. Keep in mind also that no domain is too personal or any moment too tender to invade in search of deeper truth and actual motivation.

Read just enough on psychology and psychoanalysis to acquire a vocabulary of the following items and a vague concept of their meaning: hidden hostilities, mother or father fixations, latent homosexuality, dual-personality problems, repressed desires, guilt, and inferiority complexes.

Having acquired this smattering of knowledge, you can consider yourself qualified to interpret everyone's problems, from casual acquaintances to heads of state and historical figures. Your main subjects, however, should naturally be the men you meet.

Shortly after establishing an acquaintance with a man, begin to explain him to himself with an analysis of his personality, desires, inner conflicts, ambitions, etc. Do not be discouraged by favorable first-time results. This is attributable to his probable fascination at hearing how someone else sees him (although you may be completely off base) and a certain satisfaction in noting that someone is sufficiently interested to select him for study.

When he returns for a second session, be prepared to get down to more serious analysis. You may want to begin with a farfetched theory about why he arrived when he did. Late, he lacks faith in himself and wanted to delay anticipated failure as long as possible; or he is in rebe'lion against established convention, society, and/or parental guidance. Early, he has a subconscious desire to be rejected and arrived early in an effort to be offensive and inconvenience you, thus meriting contempt. On time, he is so insecure and unsure of himself that he dares not arrive late or early for fear he would further disturb his precarious position.

If he dignifies your conclusions with a statement of disagreement, take this as positive proof that he is floundering around in a haze of confusion about his inner self. Then, calling upon the knowledge you have accumulated in your preparatory reading program, course in Psychology I, or association with armchair psychiatrists, and, bearing in mind that most if not all personality problems and maladjustments are rooted in childhood experiences, embark on a question-and-answer tour of his early life. Was he an only child? No? Were his brothers and sisters favored over him? Was his mother a strict disciplinarian, dominating the father and the whole household, or was she too permissive and overaffectionate? Did he resent his father, feel left out and rejected when his parents retired for the night? Was there any drinking problem in the family? Did his father desert the family? Were his parents too involved in pursuing business or social recognition to be bothered with him? Was there a stepfather or stepmother who poisoned his real father's or mother's mind against him?

When using this technique, remember to keep a watchful eye on his eyes and facial expression. Any time he resents a certain line of questioning, you'll generally be able to see it on his face; then pursue your line with even more vigor, convinced that his reactions indicate that you are getting uncomfortably near the heart of the matter. Since the ordinary standards of good taste and customary borders of private experiences do not have to be respected by missionaries in search of psychological truths, nothing need limit your dedicated journey into his psyche.

If, for instance, you detect that he is beginning to get serious and trying to establish the necessary romantic setting, you should become even more detached; think of yourself as the psychiatrist in charge and set about examining the subconscious motives behind his libidinous desires. Is he the classic Don Juan, constantly seeking new conquests because he is unable to be fulfilled by any of them? Does he simply want to prove something to himself and satisfy his male ego? Are you the symbol of female authority he always resented in his mother, a schoolteacher, or woman boss, and consequently seeks to destroy? Is he, unable to achieve social or business success, therefore out to set a record of sorts by winning the battle of seduction? Is he only interested in impressing his fellow rogues? Does he have a low opinion of the opposite sex and try to substantiate it whenever possible? Is he uncertain about his own masculinity and trying to establish it more securely by sexual conquest? Is he bitter, after being hurt and rejected by some girl, and trying to take it out on the entire sex?

Question him at length in order to classify him in one of the above categories (or another of your choosing) and completely destroy the romantic mood he was trying to create.

Creating a quasi-clinical atmosphere in which his romantic urges are analyzed and dissected *ad nauseam* will usually suffice to dampen the most ardent spirits. Furthermore, if you wax eloquent in your analysis and are able to go on at some length—say half an hour or more—chances are you will put your target to sleep. That unromantic, not to mention ungentlemanly, conduct is in itself reason enough to terminate the relationship without further ado.

The Last Supper (Out)

A properly planned and executed dinner outing can leave a bad taste that your target will probably not forget for years. I have found this one, if well done, a virtually foolproof rejection technique. Following are some succulent suggestions that should prove helpful in preparing such a treat. Add or subtract ingredients according to the circumstances, and season to distaste.

When a prospect invites you out to dinner, set your heart in advance on a particular restaurant, your selection depending on your victim's financial situation, personal preferences, and idiosyncrasies.

If he has limited means, insist (needless to say) on an extravagantly priced restaurant. If the prospect is wealthy and would enjoy impressing you at a deluxe spot where the maître d' would scramble to accommodate him, suggest some unpretentious little place where you can be sure no one will know or cater to him.

If he is particularly fussy, introduce him to that quaint, unconventional little restaurant where the waiter is known to lick his thumb after serving a particularly appetizing soup.

Obviously, romantic types should be guided to the bright lights to illuminate their intentions. Such an atmosphere usually darkens their mood in short order.

If your prospect has made a reservation, your plan must of course be changed. But don't despair; all is by no means lost. When you arrive at the restaurant of his choice—probably where he is known—show in every possible way that you do not fit in. Decline to check your coat, draping it around your shoulders and possibly brushing something or someone as you pass between the tables. Make yourself conspicuous, perhaps dropping something (an open purse is ideal, but anything round or rolly that is apt to disappear under a table will do).

Regardless of which table you are taken to, find it unsuitable for one reason or another. Better, wait till you are seated, then ask to change tables.

After you are settled and the waiter brings the menu, initiate a small-talk period about a friend who once worked in this restaurant, giving an account of why he said he would never eat here. Quote him: "It looks elegant, right? But you should see the kitchen. It would make the inside of a garbage can look clean."

When the waiter returns to ask if you would like to place your orders, say coldly, "I haven't had a chance to look at the menu yet." Thus chastened, he will generally be reluctant to return to the table too soon, which will afford you the opportunity to call him impatiently as he tries, hands full, to wait on another party. If you can manage it, at least one argument with the waiter should be included in each last-supper plan.

When the waiter finally returns to take your order, ask for clarification of several items. "Does the chef wash his hands before peeling the tomatoes?" "Is the champagne chilled?" "Is the sole fresh?"

After receiving the waiter's assurances or explanations, mention something completely different: *coquille maison.* When your relieved prospect assumes that this is your choice and asks what you will have with it, explain that you were only eliminating that dish (eliminate a few others in the same way). Find out what he is having. Reject that. Then ask the waiter for his recommendation. Reject that as well.

When you have finally decided on a main course, ask for a salad, then change from French dressing to Russian to Italian. This way, whichever he finally brings can turn out to be the one *from* which you changed.

Remember, too, that even if you were unable to lure your target to a restaurant visibly above his means, you can always order not by dish but by price. Order the highest-priced appetizer, the deluxe meat dish, imported French bread, endive salad (especially if they are not included in the price of the entree), and the best vintage wine. Whenever there is a question of whether or not to order dessert, always decide affirmatively. Admit you are full, but may as well have a little something sweet—which should always turn out to be the most expensive on the menu. Never finish your dessert.

Once the ordering is done, exhibit a side of your personality never before seen. Put on your brightest smile or your most sensuous look, whichever you do best—and scan the room for more likely prospects. No matter whom you are with, remember: your attitude should always be that there is someone better, if you look hard enough. If you find him, sneak sly glances in his direction when your victim is not looking. If the interested one returns your attention, strike up a visual friendship with him, increasingly ignoring your table partner.

When the food is served, try to find something to send back—to show you are accustomed only to the finest. If the wine is the best Bordeaux, take a taste and say, "Don't you find this corky?"

Watch your table manners and try to be sure they include at least one of the following: elbows on the table, gum in the ashtray, loud noises while eating your soup, buttering your bread with a spoon or fork, sucking out the last drops of liquid that has tried to hide under the ice cubes, smoking *while* eating, snuffing out your cigarette on the salad plate.

If all the above doesn't end your burgeoning relationship in jig time, conclude that your target is a complete boor, incapable of knowing good manners when he sees them, and drop him.

The Last Supper (In)

If you tire of playing the restaurant game, you may occasionally want to switch and have an intimate "last supper" at home.

A simple dinner, with steaks or chops, green vegetable, potatoes, and salad can be more or less counted on to turn out successfully. Therefore, eliminate such menus in favor of complicated or fancy dishes, preferably ones you have never prepared before. Rationalize this decision by telling yourself your target could get an ordinary meal any place.

You really want to impress him. Surely, you are at least as intelligent as the average cook, etc.

For exotic menu suggestions, turn to one of the women's magazines or one of the complicated French or gourmet cookbooks in which you will always find interesting ideas and long recipes. Rare dishes and six-page recipes are especially recommended since they give you two possibilities of failure: first, that it will not turn out successfully, and second, that if it does he will not like it. (One alternate possibility is to choose a casserole dish consisting of meat and vegetables, spiced heavily; if it turns out unsuccessfully, there will be nothing left to eat but the bread and butter.)

A further advantage of serving complex foreign dishes is that if he does not like them you can insinuate that he is not *au courant*, then discuss in detail the many gourmets and *bons vivants* you have cooked for in the past with *grand succès*. Contrast them to the provincial, unsophisticated types whose tastes are insufficiently developed to appreciate fine foods.

Even if you are an excellent cook and find it hard to foul up in the kitchen, you can with careful study devise ways to get to a man's nerves instead of to his heart through his stomach.

After inviting him to dinner, warn him not to eat anything at all before coming and stress the importance of his being on time. Then choose a dish that requires long preparation, and start in on it only shortly before your prospect is due to arrive. To make things even better, add loneliness to injury and hunger by selecting a preparation that will keep you in the kitchen stirring, beating, or folding-in ingredients while he sits in the living room alone.

Another good ploy is to stop the preparation and leave the kitchen to engage in political arguments, make jealous accusations, or revive past differences. If you can get sufficiently involved, dinner will almost always burn. Or choose this moment to make a protracted phone call, as ominous odors and thickening smoke begin to invade the living room.

After your target has spent at least half an hour in the living room alone, you can relent and let him join you in the kitchen. Then, feel free to perform such aesthetic gestures as wiping the knife on your apron, smoothing loose hairs into place just before kneading or forming patties, checking the seasoning by sipping from or licking the stirring spoon.

At the table (assuming you ever get there) show how interested you are in your dinner partner by carefully observing his progress with any exotic food from which he seems to be shying away.

In a motherly way, call his attention to the fact that he has hardly touched his okra or that he's allowing the broiled brains to get cold. After you have coaxed him to finish something he obviously regards as less than a favorite, overrule his objections and give him another generous portion. Grow offended if he does not clean his plate.

Sometimes the menu should be determined according to your target's job or professional field. If he is a doctor or in some business where his hours must be flexible because of something that could arise unexpectedly, select dishes accordingly. Fluffy omelettes, soufflés, puff pastries with gravy fillings, and other things that fall or become soggy and ruined if they are not served immediately are good choices. In this way, if he comes late, not only will he find dinner a mess, he will also find an argument all ready and waiting—because it is all his fault.

Last suppers at home are a satisfying rejection technique not only because they work wonders but also because they leave you with a good conscience after the disaster. You've worked and slaved over a hot stove for the bastard, and look at the thanks you get. Clearly, such an unappreciative, uncouth prospect is undeserving of you.

156

XXX

Horizontal Alienation, or How to Get the Intercourse Off Course

If till now we have dealt with basically social situations—what I term the "vertical"—here we will offer a few pregnant analyses and suggestions regarding a word as short as it is powerful: sex. Never, but never, underestimate the alienation powers of sex. It is, without doubt, your most important tool—the ultimate weapon to be used when all else fails.

The male assumption that bed is at the end of the evening can be turned by any reasonably neurotic female into a technique so immediately alienating that all others pale before it.* From this basic premise has evolved Kennedy's

* For those of you who protest that your male friends are not so one-tracked (or obsessed), let me say that my experience and research have

157

Fourth Corollary: In the realm of the horizontal, the degree of alienation is directly proportional to the man's desire.

Sex is the area in which men are most vulnerable. The extremes to which they go, the indignities they endure, the sacrifices they make in the pursuit of sex are unparalleled. But it is not enough simply to be aware of this potential. Women must learn the techniques for harnessing and channeling this force for their own negative ends. They must learn how to lessen their sexual desirability, minimize a man's pleasure during sex, spoil the climax, and—if worse has come to worst and sex has, despite all efforts, proved enjoyable—how to minimize the postcoitus effects.

Following are several highly recommended approaches for achieving excellent negative results. They are applicable whether you believe in sex at first sight, with the more frequent rejection fulfillment this may afford; only after a "reasonable" time; or simply as a last resort.

The Cold Fish Approach

In the view of virtually all men queried, there is no more unappetizing dish than the Cold Fish. Indeed, she has probably evoked more overall negative responses and turned off more men, than any other.

It remains to be proved whether Cold Fish are born or made. But if you happened to have grown up steeped in the sex-is-filthy (or too shocking to mention) tradition; or were influenced by the hell-and-damnation, fire-and-brimstone, sex-and-passion-corrupt-the-soul teachings of some

---

revealed beyond any shadow of doubt that behind every dinner or theater invitation, behind every symposium (or podium of any sort), any concert or even movie, lies the bed. He claims he likes you for your mind? Nonsense! To him, "mind" is a four-letter word. And he's interested in another one.

religions, you obviously start with a definite advantage.*
Even if you have had a fairly normal background, however, there is no reason for you to be deprived of the rejection potential CF has to offer. For example, you might
overidentify with a favorite aunt—or even your mother—
who endured a tearful, constantly degrading relationship.
Concentrate on the depressing consequences of such a
union, and vow to keep your defenses up at all costs to
avoid similar degradation and hurt.

Or try to build up your Bitterness Reserve. If (as is
probably the case) you have had an especially painful and
heartbreaking love affair of your own, hark back to it constantly. Let us suppose, for instance, that though you were
firmly convinced that the divine man involved loved you,
and that though you unstintingly extended yourself for
him, he later dropped you unceremoniously.

For months, or even years, after the termination of your
unhappy relationship, regularly take time out to sit down
and recall in living color every depressing detail of what
transpired. Remember again how perfect he seemed at
first, and how much you trusted him. Relive every sacrifice
you made for him, and the terrible humiliations you expe-
rienced when your family and friends found out what a
fool you had been. If you have friends in common, torture
yourself by questioning them whenever possible about his
new (and seemingly very satisfactory) life with someone
else. If you know the places he frequents, waste time
scheming about how to get to them—perhaps with someone else, to "make him jealous," though obviously he
couldn't care less.

If you want to contribute even more to your Bitterness
Reserve, try going to the neighborhood where he now

* A beautiful divorcée, introduced to me as being burdened with some of
the most incapacitating sexual hang-ups in history, later confided to me
that she was considering suing her church for what she felt was its responsibility for inducing them.

lives and hide out in a nearby building, or behind a car down the street, waiting for him and his true love to come out together. You will often find that this comparatively minimal effort will supply you with sufficient acrid nutriment to feed your neurosis for months to come.

It is unlikely that one unhappy love affair, no matter how neurotically handled, can in itself result in your becoming a Cold Fish, but remember: you have to start somewhere. Dwelling neurotically on even a single romantic disaster can sometimes produce the equivalent Bitterness Reserve of half a dozen "normal" heartbreaks.

In order for you to ascertain at which point you have become a functioning Cold Fish, or how far along you are in the right direction, I offer below the Standard Cold Fish Test. It was composed on the basis of a twenty-year study of Cold Fish tales and statistics compiled by a veritable army of researchers:

1. Do you dislike the use of endearing names for yourself or others, considering them too embarrassing, or phony?

2. For some reason, do you sense an inexplicable tension any time sex is discussed in any context?

3. Even though you may submit to sexual relations with someone you feel you love, do you feel—deep down inside—that sex is dirty, and would be happier if you could enjoy the relationship without sexual involvement?

4. Does it get on your nerves to be stroked, caressed (what you may call "pawed") even by someone you otherwise like?

5. Do you feel you are being taken advantage of during sex?

6. Do your customary icy bearings only thaw to coincide with your plan to request a financial or other favor from someone?

7. Are you convinced that sex is vastly overrated?

8. Have you always found that you are too uptight to

have a climax (even with someone you recognize is appealing and competent)?

9. Do you have a cavalier, surrender-on-demand attitude toward sex, not because you are relaxed about it but because it is "of no importance to you"?

10. Do you have a distorted idea about or preoccupation with hygiene that makes your devotion to germ warfare supersede your desire for sexual satisfaction?

11. Do you have the "lofty notion" that the only true purpose of sex is procreation, and that it is debasing to participate in it for any other reason?

12. Are you aggressively defensive any time you meet someone new, because you meticulously keep the details of all past disappointments uppermost in your mind?

In scoring, consider yourself suspect if you answer any two of the above questions affirmatively. If three or more answers are "yes," you qualify as a fledgling CF. Congratulations!

The Limited Commitment Plan

Although this approach is called the Limited Commitment Plan, the opportunities it provides for rejection gratification are virtually limitless. It is particularly subscribed to and dearly cherished by those women who, although basically responsive to the idea of having sex, are not fully committed to the fulfillment.

Their reservations may be imputed to a number of things, but most, I have found, grow out of a fundamental sense of insecurity and a fear that the target may not come back after he has "had his way" with them. Other bases are: the brevity of an acquaintance; an impression that the man's financial or attendance record may not yet entitle him to such intimacies; a sneaking suspicion that he may be married or "only out for what he can get"; the fact that a bad reputation precedes him; a strategy to convince him that nothing valuable comes easy; or an unfortunate post-sex result with a similar type.

However, instead of delaying their submission until such time as they feel they are on solid ground—or firm bed—they yield at a time or place they suspect will be premature or otherwise ill-advised. Consequently, they are able to surrender under duress, by withholding to various degrees full cooperation, setting forth unreasonable conditions, and making unpalatable demands.

Thus, they have on the one hand a certain satisfaction in knowing that the victor did not come by his spoils easily, that he had to "sweat for it," and, on the other hand, their attitude can alienate perfectly well-intentioned prospects. The unfulfilling, confusing, and often arduous sexual experience that the Limited Commitment Plan provides often leaves a man frustrated or even hostile after sex.

If this plan appeals to you—and I hope it does—here are some of the methods through which it can be implemented.

The Here or Nowhere Impasse

This is a timeworn but trusty technique whereby, though you agree to perform in the sex scene, you refuse to accompany the male protagonist to a suitable staging area. His persistent attempts to coax, cajole, entreat, or even trick you into repairing to a proper setting are to no avail, as are his cogent arguments to prove the infeasibility of starting the production in cramped quarters, semiprivate surroundings, or places where interruptions could occur at any moment.

After it becomes clear that you will not be budged, most men will, in the best show-must-go-on tradition, give up and start things in the take-it-or-leave-it location you have chosen: on your living room sofa (though your roommate's schedule is unclear); at the end of the hall (where there is no place to lie down); in his tiny sports car; on the apartment staircase.

To justify your behavior on a conscious level (though you are fully aware subconsciously that it is self-defeating and counterproductive), tell yourself it's only because you're convinced that sex in the heat of the moment is more moral than premeditated sex. Or try to convince yourself that you're doing what you're doing where you're doing it because you think your partner will enjoy it more—despite repeated pleas to the contrary.*

Almost invariably, you will find that sex dramas "laid" under these exasperating conditions will be doomed to failure. Remember too: the more outlandish the scene or setting, the more rejection techniques you can bring into play to ruin the sex scene and place the corresponding blame on the hapless target.

The Verbal Overkill Technique

Not even the most brilliant nuclear scientists, with the most advanced technological knowledge, could conceive of a device more effective for exploding the mood of the sex scene than the device known as VOK—verbal overkill. Even if you consider yourself a veteran in the field of destructive conversational techniques, and possessed of the expertise to talk yourself out of the graces of most prospects before half the evening has passed, I recommend the following to your attention for their specific destructive effects in the sex arena.

The next time you find yourself being lovingly conducted toward the commencement of the first act with someone who shows no signs of wanting to reject you, become nervous. Begin to ask yourself suspiciously: Why

---

* Naturally, if there is any remote indication that the man involved would actually enjoy getting it on the sneak, this whole project must be abandoned forthwith.

would he want me? How long can this sweetness and light last—especially after the mystery is gone? What am I letting myself in for now? This will help get you out of the mood and divert your partner as well from his obvious course. Start talking, keeping the subject matter as unrelated and incompatible with the business at hand as possible. For example, if you have already asked him his astrological sign (and told him you had guessed it right even before he told you), begin to expound at length on it. Cite all the great men throughout history who were born under the same sign, and detail their lives wherever possible. Talk so fast that he cannot get a word in edgewise to try to get the conversation off the stars and back down to earth.

Be on the alert for any sly attempt he may make to employ double entendres to bring the question of sex back into the picture before he grows too mind-weary to care.

By the time he finally engineers the subject back to sex, the act itself—if indeed it happens—should be anticlimactic. You will not need to consult your horoscope to know that ultimate rejection is a virtual certainty.

Controversy Bombs have long been favorite weapons with rejection seekers the world over. Much advice has already been offered on how to use this ploy in vertical situations. Let me stress, however, that controversy—especially heated—is also a sure-fire tool for cooling off the sex scene.

The Liquid Path to Rejection

Considering the many points in favor of having a few drinks, it is always easy to justify the idea. After all, an evening over cocktails or a bottle of wine is almost always the "groovier" for it. Too, drinking is both relaxing and stimulating (though it is said to be a depressant). Besides, alcohol helps release inhibitions, or provides an excuse for releasing them.

With these positive aspects in mind, buy a bottle of your favorite alcoholic drink on the evening of your big date with a promising new target. (Ignore the fact that you know things take a turn for the worse when you drink.) As soon as you get home, relax and have a few. You might even want to start the ball rolling (downhill, of course) by beginning to drink at lunchtime, especially if you are anxious to appear composed when you meet him, or if you have certain financial, romantic, or family problems that you would like to "forget" by evening (if you look hard enough you can always find a reason).

You may have noticed that while most men tend to encourage you to relax and have a drink or two—thereby intending to lower your resistance—there is a point of diminishing returns. As you reach then pass it, your appeal will usually decrease proportionately.

Since no negative reaction is likely to be obtained if you can drink without having it interfere with your personality, judgment, or general equilibrium, here are some drinking tips to bear in mind:

1. Become hostile and aggressive. Make up your mind that you will not let anyone tell you when you have had enough. (After all, you are of age, and probably self-supporting, so how dare he presume to establish liquid-consumption standards for you?) If he persists in his holier-than-thou attitude or offends you in any way, remember: four-letter words are often the most succinct and explicit way to make a point.

2. Become giddy and giggly. Shower your date with a stream of titters and cackles. Every time he tries to get romantic, laugh and dig out some off-color jokes. If he tries to quiet you down, say, "That's precisely what's wrong with the world today. Some people hate to see anyone having a good time." Tell him not to be so uptight, to "get with it," and if he stubbornly remains morose and critical, get on the phone and call someone with a decent sense of humor. Whisper and laugh over the phone, while he waits.

3. Become tearful and maudlin. There is nothing like a crying jag to dampen the love nest. If alcohol makes you feel dejected, think of something sad (perhaps the problem that you were drinking to forget) and begin to talk and weep at the same time about it. If your target is even mildly sympathetic, let it inspire you to an even better performance. Be inconsolable if he tries to comfort you . . . he just doesn't understand . . . or he really doesn't care about you. (This will also satisfy the frustrated actress in you.)

Try to establish—while dabbing eyes and vigorously blowing your nose—whether he really likes you or is only using you like all the others. (If you don't use this approach *before sex,* try it during or after.)

4. Become sloppy and disheveled. Since concern about your appearance can also be dispensed with once you have overindulged, turn slovenly as soon as possible. If you get hungry, eat standing up, designating all foods finger foods and napkins an unnecessary accessory; lick any excess food off your fingers, or wipe it on whatever you're wearing. If he makes you coffee, perhaps in a last-ditch effort to save something of the relationship in spite of you, refuse to drink it, perceiving that it may be part of a conspiracy to get you sober. If he tries to reason with you, push the coffee away, if possible hard enough to spill some. Preferably on him.

When you stagger into the bedroom, disregard the fact that your hair is a mess, your stockings falling, your makeup smeared (no one is perfect), and expect Romeo to swing into action the moment you present yourself on the bed.

Timing

The significance of proper timing has long been recognized by those in divergent occupations from comedians to generals. If you can acquire the knack for the right kind of bad timing, the demolition of even the most romantic mood cannot be far behind. Let us suppose, for example, that you are with your co-star in some perfectly staged setting. The house lights are dim, soft music is playing, your target is clearly throbbing with desire. At this crucial moment, call an unscheduled intermission. For instance, explain apologetically that you are not wearing your diaphragm (suppository, vaginal foam, or whatever) and will have to go and fetch it.

Or simply get up, change an album that may have been playing over and over, close the blinds, or turn down the lights. (If you are among those who feel that sex is acceptable only when performed in pitch darkness, you could stop proceedings at this critical point to extinguish every light, perhaps even drawing the heavy drapes to prevent any sliver of street light from penetrating the room. This is particularly recommended when the target has expressed a clear preference for some degree of lighting.)

By the time you return to the matters so abruptly interrupted, the mood will usually be broken . . . and so will your prospect's spirit.

Staging the Preliminary Wrestling Bout

It is generally recognized that one of the deadliest snakes in the garden of sexual fulfillment is exhaustion, especially on the part of the male. Small wonder, then, that pre-sex tactics, meant to wear a man out and leave him so weary at the beginning of the act that he can hardly function, are so popular with successful failures everywhere.

One of the favored methods for assuring that a man will be exhausted before sex is to engage him in a pre-sex wrestling bout. If this notion appeals to you, remember that the best frustration results when the man has the greatest incentive, inspiration, and hope of winning. It is up to you to provide this illusion by convincing him early on that your basic sensuous, exciting nature makes you a worthy "purse," and that victory is well within his grasp.

The next time you are with a good prospect who wants to engage you in a sex match, respond eagerly on a physical level using your best techniques, offering only feeble, half-hearted reasons why you can't, or shouldn't. This will indicate to your adversary that all that stands between him and gratification is overcoming your limited objections and reducing your already crumbling defenses.

In the beginning he will probably rely on his powers of persuasion. As he outlines his position detailing why you should accede to his demands, pretend to be in complete agreement with him—almost. Concede that he may be right, but suggest that it might be a little too soon. Or tell him you want to but are not quite sure it would be the right thing to do. Or you might promise him to yield if only he will wait until the following night, or if you could be sure he would come back after you "give in." Since it is difficult for the target to deal with these questions and statements on a logical basis, he will usually waste no more time but swing into the physical aspect of his pre-sex workout.

In this phase he will hold you close, whispering sweet and reassuring nothings (the standard things about how much he likes you, how much he wants and needs you, how wonderful it will be for the two of you as he strokes and caresses you). Now seem to be persuaded; pretend that your defenses are crumbling, by making your objections more halting, less defined. Say, "Well . . . I don't know," adding a few well-placed sighs, which will signal to him that the bout is all but over. (Little does he know: it has hardly begun!)

At this point, allow him fairly free rein (the emphasis is on "fairly"), but stop him every time he makes any move to get down to the actual business at hand. Wriggle, squirm, and firmly resist when he tries to remove any piece of your clothing.* Whenever he tries to make the final "contact," scramble free. As you slide, jump, and turn in the bed, make meaningless conversation. Say, "Oh, you're terrible!" Or, "Can't you wait just a minute?" Or you might ask him what he's trying to do, as if it were not abundantly clear. Giggle like a schoolgirl in her first tumble, in response to his attempt to be more masterful. If he tries to force things, squeal and lurch away as if you were "goosey" in that spot. Do not eliminate the possibility of having to spring out of bed, with him in hot pursuit.

Continue this workout until you see the sweat on his brow, or until his desperate tone suggests rape, assault, or retreat. (If your determination shows signs of weakening at any time prior to seeing such signs, remember last year's encounter with that darling fellow who *swore* you were just the type of girl he had always hoped he'd meet some day and even managed to squeeze out a few stray tears at the thought of your not trusting him. And what did he do after you lowered your defenses to permit him to touch your heart . . . and other parts?)

Only when your opponent shows signs of utter frustration and first-degree fatigue do you lower your guard and let him penetrate your defenses. At this point he will probably be so worn out he will feel more like going into his corner and collapsing than beginning a sex match. Conversely, if you have been sufficiently titillating as you teased, he may be so aroused that an embarrassing knockout-climax might occur when he has barely commenced the first round. In either case, *you* will have been in control—heady stuff—and when he quits the ring, ego damaged and understandably resentful, the likelihood of his requesting a return bout are remote indeed.

---

* Unlike the Limited Commitment Girl, who is firm in her resolve to go only so far, make it obvious—or seemingly obvious—here that you are wavering, as though waiting for his guidance.

The Free-Love Approach

The Free-Love Approach is enthusiastically endorsed and promoted by men. The theory is that sex, like eating, sleeping, and other bodily functions, should be performed easily, naturally, and indiscriminately, with all comers. Women who espouse the plan tend to equate sex with love, and believe that through repeated affairs they are fulfilling—or stand a chance of fulfilling "next time"—their need for love and affection. Other proponents like the approach because they equate sex with power—a power wielded only during the sex drama, because of the unquestionable significance of their position at such times. And in other cases—though medical evidence to support it is minimal—the women in question claim to be driven by implacable sex drives.

Whatever the reason used to justify the approach, it can with a bit of deft maneuvering be turned into an excellent rejection technique.

One word of warning, however: surrender on demand is advisable only for those who hope to prejudice their roles with the male protagonist involved. Statitics show that nine of ten men oppose free love—when practiced by the "weaker sex." What of that elusive tenth? By the time you meet the divinely mature tenth man who appreciates your warmth and honesty, who admires your lack of complexity and accepts your instant gift in the manner it was intended, you are usually too neurotic—from the nine rejections—to relate to him in any meaningful way.

The attitude of most men toward practitioners of free sex is doubtless a result of their inability to free themselves from values learned at mother's knee, or the cumbersome shackles of convention. Or it could be that what Freud described as man's naturally combatant and possessive nature is responsible, since it makes victory without challenge seem less appealing. At any rate, most men regard such practitioners as unstable, or an easy mark at best, and immoral to boot. We have, then, the paradoxical situation wherein men work, connive, and plot to attain sexual fulfillment but at the same time are harsh and sometimes pitiless judges of women who grant them what they seek too quickly. Even as men encourage they are preparing to condemn.

Here are some of the blandishments you can expect to hear from men bent on fostering the free-love concept. As you hear them echoing in your mind, know how quickly they will be followed by the terrible swift sword—which is what you really want, isn't it?

1. It is not the length of time two people have known each other that counts, but what they feel for each other. (You are usually allowed a few extra minutes to make this all-important evaluation.)

2. If you don't think enough of him to see that he is sincere, that he is no fly-by-night fraud interested only in momentary sexual fulfillment, he may as well forget the whole thing. (Don't ask the fate of the other girls with whom he was "sincere.")

3. You are so irresistible and his desire for you so compelling that he can't bear to be in your presence without possessing you. (In other words: "Let's get sex out of the way so I can relax or it's all over before it begins.")

4. You are what he has always been looking for—he thinks—but he will be certain only after sex.

5. His only reason for wanting to have sex is for your sake . . . he wants to treat you to a pleasure more exquisite than any you have ever known.

6. It is ridiculous to observe seventeenth-century Puritanical values in the twentieth century (although he doubtless will when he becomes "serious," and chooses someone to present to mother).

7. Since you are no longer a virgin, there is no reason to "make a big fuss" about another affair. (Now that you're "used" or "no good," you may as well have an open-leg policy.)

8. Old maids are almost all virgins, withered but untouched. (Don't be so "fresh" tonight because you too are perishable; in other words: give it up before it wilts.)

9. The warmth and beauty of that precious moment may never be recaptured if allowed to escape. (Many instant lovers vanish as quickly as precious moments.)

10. After all, he will be "giving" his body just as you will be giving yours. (Even proceeding from this premise, if both parties give the same, why should one have the right to determine the best moment, or push so much harder to make his "equal" contribution?)

The High-Risk-Sex Co-Star

For women unreceptive to the idea of instant sex, alternative approaches are needed. One of these, quite popular because it usually affords as reliable insurance against development of serious relations as does instant sex, yet allows a girl to maintain some sense of morality, involves choosing the high-risk-sex co-star.

Very simply, this involves teaming up with an improbable sex partner, preferably someone you have been seeing irregularly and who is odds-out nonfavored to prove serious. If you exercise the right kind of bad judgment in making your choice, even if all goes well before and after sex, the chances for further involvement are slim.

Here are some of the telltale signs that can help you recognize the high-risk-sex co-star:

1. He usually calls you at the last minute (perhaps with tickets to a play he has obviously had for some time or an invitation to accompany him to a party at the eleventh hour).

2. He is not interested in anything concerning you or your accomplishments, nor does he confide anything to you about his plans, preferring to center all conversations around sex—when you are going to say yes, or serve seconds, thirds, fourths, and so on.

3. Citing one excuse or another, he always seems to be tied up and unavailable on holidays, weekends, and other important days when "best girls" are customarily given preference.

4. He appears reluctant to spend money on you, though he lavishes all manner of luxury on himself.

5. He invariably fails to call back after you have had sex with him, claiming to have been busy or out of town (he never bothered to send so much as a postcard).

6. Whenever he takes you out, it is to out-of-the-way places or after-hours joints; also, there is no place where you can contact him; you have never met any of his friends, and he is unwilling to meet any of yours.

7. He admits to having a girl friend or wife, but claims that the relationship is very unsatisfactory and that he likes you better and would be willing to break up with the other person if he could be more sure of you (the proof of the pudding is in sex). Or, if the relationship is already on a sexual "footing," he wants you to continue to submit because the actual star for whom you are the sexual stand-in cannot fulfill his physical needs as well as you can. . . . And he is trying to get out of the other, only searching for a "delicate" way.

8. Any time you want to plan something with him, he has to "let you know," and usually he "lets you know" that for some reason or another he will not be able to make it.

9. He tells you "frankly" that he doesn't plan to get serious with anyone, but if you want to "have a good time" he's all for that. (Stud anyone?)

Making the Main Event a Flop

Let us again assume the worst, however, and suppose that all pre-sex attempts have failed, and that one arrives at the main event with the target intact, seemingly very much on top of things. Still, all is not lost. The sensitive nature of the sex act itself makes it an ideal situation for you to upset the delicate balance, and literally wreak havoc.

Few things can have as decisive an influence on the course and outcome of a production as the background music accompanying it. The right theme can greatly inspire a performer, while the wrong one can prove so insidious it can ruin the entire event.

One popular "tune" that lends itself especially well to the latter purpose is the "I shouldn't be doing this" refrain. For best results, it should be introduced into the background at the most inopportune times possible, i.e., when the male performer is clearly trying to concentrate on the rapturous drama in progress, or when he is attempting to deliver his most soul-stirring lines. At such times, take inspiration from the theme song and begin murmuring, "I shouldn't be doing this." Or, "I've never done anything like this before." (Even though you may have done the same thing the previous night and a thousand nights before, you need not hesitate; the effect will be the same.)

When distrust is involved, make the lament more personal. Say, "I shouldn't be doing this with you." Or, "I guess I won't hear from you any more after tonight." Or try, "I guess you think I do this with everybody." And if disappointment and dissatisfaction with the performance is the key to your feeling, try, "I knew I shouldn't have done this . . . I knew it would be a mistake."

Another distracting and destructive technique is to comment impatiently on your partner's performance during sex. What you want to get across in so many words is: "I wish the hell you'd hurry up and get through." However, in the interest of diplomacy and in order to keep up the pretense of trying not to discourage a man whom you feel on a conscious level you do not want to alienate, a more tactful approach is recommended, at least at first. Say, "How much longer are you going to be?" Or, "Come on, darling, stop dawdling!"

The problem, of course, is that such lines may cool the

mood and even further delay the ending. (This is particularly true when you begin your questions early on, trying to establish how much longer it will be when he has barely started.) At any rate, if in spite of your gentle nudging he still proves uncooperative, you will naturally have to be a trifle more emphatic. Say curtly, "I wish you'd hurry up and finish!" Or, if you're feeling really mean, "Are you still in?"

With anyone who does not respond to these admonitions you can build and become even more blunt: "What're you trying to do, wear me out?" Or attack him; say, "Something must be wrong with you!" If you make it a practice to spend as much time as possible during the sex act asking barbed questions and making catty remarks instead of relaxing and enjoying it, chances are you will ruin his performance and enjoyment. Do not hesitate to use this tactic even though you may have earlier responded to your partner and been satisfied by him. After that, begin to lose interest, now apparently totally indifferent as to whether or not he finds fulfillment in his performance.

A girl who does not keep her mind on her work can frequently strike the kind of off-key, abstract note that invariably takes its toll, affecting both the mood of the act and the spirit of the male performer. The more irrelevant or unrelated the comment, the better. If things are progressing nicely, say, "Oh, dear, I think my car's illegally parked. Could you check?" Or, if you have a cat or dog, choose an especially tender moment to interrupt: "I wonder if I fed Minou (or Fido)."

Ambiguity can also prove devastating. One I have found a sure-fire alienating procedure is a whispered, "Oh my God!" Then, lest your target get the impression that you are merely beginning to feel your part, repeat, with a note of disgust, "Oh my God!" When he interrupts things to determine the cause of your apparent concern, explain that you just remembered that you left the air-conditioning on in your office. If this does not seem to have killed the mood and he dismisses your worry as baseless, don't let go. Say, "What happens when an air-conditioner is left on over the weekend?" Or, "Do you think I ought to try and contact the night watchman?"

You can also interrupt the production and destroy the mood by sounding notes of alarm. "Be quiet a moment. . . . Didn't you hear something by the door? . . . No, wait. . . . I think I heard footsteps." Choose a delicate moment to say, "I think I smell something burning." (Especially good if neither of you smokes.) If he is the type who would be cool and self-controlled in a fire, here is one that rarely fails to give him pause even in this age of the pill: "Suppose I get pregnant after all this?"

If for any reason the above distracting interjections do not appeal to you, you can achieve the same effect by going to the other extreme and feigning passions you do not feel. As it happens, even men who have little sense of rhythm, harmony, or sincerity usually detect any such phony notes. If you can convince yourself that you are cleverer than most men, that people believe what they want to believe, and that flattery will get you anyplace, it should be easy for you to utilize this technique.

As you sense his temperature rising, pretend yours is escalating too ("Yes, my darling, yes!"). Begin to breathe hard (half as many breaths, but twice as deeply). If you have always suspected that you could have been a great actress had you not been bogged down in your present job, you may want to sound a few well-chosen spoken lines. Variations on the "Oh-darling-you-make-me-feel-wonderful" or "I-never-knew-it-was-possible-to-feel-such-pleasure" clichés are especially good. Also, burning pleas, or fiery demands that he *never stop* making love to you have been proven disconcerting when they are obviously insincere. Even poorly placed "Ohs," "Ahs," "Ummms," and "Ohhs" (not to mention squeals of pleasure and delight) can produce their effect.

If you think you have a real flair for drama, you may feel

inclined to try the four-letter ploy. It is inspired by the opinion, prevalent in many circles, that the perfect woman is the one who can be a lady in the living room and a whore in the bedroom. Intone explicit descriptions of what is taking place, leaving nothing to the imagination; reveal what you are feeling, where, and why.

The four-letter ploy is especially recommended if you know your partner is sensitive to such terms. Or if he has mentioned the possibility of studying for the ministry.

Assuming the Director's Role: General Techniques

While a large segment of the male population may consider a certain amount of initiative in a woman stimulating, if she overdoes it and takes full charge, especially during first performances, she leaves herself open for possible double jeopardy. First, not knowing a man's preferences on "opening night," she has more opportunity, as the director, to lead the drama off course. And second, many men in principle resent having their roles completely usurped.

If you want to assume a director's role, there are two basic approaches. First, you can take over from the beginning (implying a lack of faith in your co-performer and in his ability to conduct the production to a successful conclusion). Bases for this are: you believe that he has not had as much experience as you; that he seems clumsy; that he would not be likely to determine your sexual needs, or even realize his own as fully, without your direction. Or second, you can appropriate the role to yourself in mid-performance (the implication being that you are dissatisfied with events up to that point and want to alter them), which we shall discuss separately.

If you assume control from the beginning, give free rein to your imagination, to make sure that what happens under your direction is different—real dynamite. After all, by taking over you imply that you can get more out of the performance than he could; thus it would be rather pointless to follow beaten paths or the customary routine.

However, this need to avoid the more traditional procedures might lead you to direct acts about which you have certain reservations or fears. To help you overcome them, here is a helpful list of theories and rationalizations relied on by millions of women to sustain them in their unconventional choices:

1. Nothing in sex is dirty; only people's minds are dirty.

2. Since what we consider perverted in this society is considered normal in others, no one has a basis for making a definitive judgment.

3. Putting limits on sex is for hardhats, not sophisticates.

4. All sexual appetites are normal; no sexual activity between consenting adults should concern anyone else.

5. Some of the greatest evangelists for purity and conformity in sex, stability of the family, and law and order in society are often hiding their hang-ups behind their public pronouncements.

6. Some of the world's most talented and creative people have been sexual nonconformists.

7. One man's meat is another man's poison.

8. Whatever the *other* fellow likes is perverted.

Now that you have seen that no sexual experience—not even group sex in Macy's window—need necessarily be repressed or eliminated, you have only to decide which kind of so-called unorthodox sexual activity you will direct. First, of course, you must determine, if you don't already know, what kind of target you're dealing with.

If, for example, he is an obvious sexual conservative, who squirms and shows discomfort at the movies any time sex scenes become too graphic, whose imagination in sex seems to extend from A to B, whose forte is gentle kisses from well-pursed lips, you may decide that what he needs is a sexual awakening. Convince yourself that he is actually smoldering just beneath the surface, secretly eager to release his long pent-up emotions. (After all, how does he know what he will like before he tries it?)

Having thus assessed the situation, shortly after you hit the bed the first time, dart under the covers and begin demonstrating your mastery of advanced fellatio techniques. With this for openers, move on to other things; avoiding cracks and crevices some ill-informed people regard as filthy is only "copping out." Besides, didn't you read in the popular sex manuals that this was the way to drive a man mad—for you?

Remember, too, that turnabout is fair play, and when it becomes clear that he has no intention of kissing anything below the bottom of your chin, manipulate your body into a position whereby he will either have to demonstrate the extent of his lingual ability or quickly turn his head.

Consider the possibility of directing your sexually conservative co-star to incorporate vibrators, frankfurters, bananas, or similar articles into the act. You'll be amazed at the shock power of one little banana!

For less conservative targets you must of course select more novel approaches in order to appear too "far out." Remember, though, that if these methods are to work effectively, it is important that they be used early in a relationship, not only for the reasons already indicated but also because, after confidence is established and sex becomes more routine, even techniques and methods generally considered very unconventional may well be welcomed . . . and could therefore backfire.

In your role as director with less conservative, more sophisticated types you might consider inviting a friend over for a *ménage à trois*. Or you might surprise and show him how avant-garde you are by inviting several friends in for an evening of swinging and swapping. If he's really interested in you, this ploy might get the jealous scene going. In which case, you know how to handle him. Then, too, the introduction of another person or persons into your sex scene always opens up the possibility that your target will find someone he likes better in the crowd.

Assuming the Director's Role: Midperformance

In taking over the direction of a scene already in progress, you may want to borrow a page or two from the book of my friend Dr. Lulu Rosenkrantz entitled *Sex and the Lively Woman, or Staying on Top of Things*. As Dr. Rosenkrantz so rightly points out, women have for too long ignored the power they hold in their hands when it comes to the sex act. What is more, she notes, while men are very much on top of the world outside of bed, *in* bed women can very quickly and authoritatively take command. One of the basic techniques she recommends is to hark back to some earlier target—whom you have doubtless long since alienated but who in retrospect looks pretty good, at least from the sexual point of view. Recall nostalgically some particularly pleasurable moment you shared with him, some caress or endearment you remember fondly, and constantly compare these moments frozen in time—and therefore memorable—with the clumsy antics of the present clod. As to timing, it is always preferable that you wait until the protagonist (you should not yet think of him an *ant*agonist) is convinced he is performing like old Don Juan himself. At which point, and in a businesslike or professorial tone, assume your directorial chores forthwith. The following dialogue should be taken solely for what it is—a guideline. You should of course personalize it and make it your own.

YOU (*gently at first, but more and more businesslike*): Darling, I wonder if you could remove your right arm from under me and prop yourself up on your elbows so you won't be a dead weight?

HE (*slightly taken aback by this untimely interruption, and taking a rather dim view of his eager person being re-*

ferred to as a "dead weight"): Oh, uh . . . sure, honey. (*He quickly complies.*)

YOU (*allowing a short time lapse, to lull him back into a false sense of security*): Darling, I wonder . . .

HE (*tenderly*): Go ahead, say it.

YOU: It's just that . . . do you . . . uh . . .

HE: What? (*In general, his tone by now will be quite strident.*)

YOU: Do you know any other movements?

If at this point he's still with you—and many a target has been known to bite the dust at this point alone—go on:

YOU: Maybe you could try to make a more . . . I don't know . . . circular movement. More like this (*taking his lower torso, try to guide and maneuver him in some more intricate and complex movement, perhaps after having confided that whatever he had been doing had, frankly, been getting monotonous*).

HE (*still aiming to please*): Something like this? (*His movement now will probably be some weird and jerky routine more appropriate to a voodoo ritual than a bed bout, despite all your manual efforts and help.*)

YOU: Well . . . (*letting your voice trail off*). The problem is, your pace is off. Too fast (*now is a good time to bring some ex-BF out into the open, using his name if your current target knows him or of him, saying*): I don't know quite how to explain it. But George was a real *master* of the motion. Wow!

That "Wow!" may well bring the bout to an end by itself, but if your target persists, or perhaps really likes you so much that all you've done to date has still not produced the desired effect, and he responds with something such as:

HE (*obviously trying to comply and at the same time recapture the romantic mood that has been shattered*): I only want to please you, darling . . .

then you have no choice but to retort:

181

YOU (*coldly*): You've slipped off your elbows again. I'm sorry, but you're really very heavy on me.

If none of the above has yet produced what I might term a withering effect, there are of course the old standbys:

1. If he is going at it hot and heavy, and has been for some time, ask, "Are you *in* yet?"

2. In the same situation, but somewhat further along, ask, "Are you finished?"

If all that precedes still doesn't unplug your friend, then you may safely assume that he is some sort of male masochist and you'd be better rid of him before he makes creepy demands on your lovely person.

The Doing-Him-a-Big-Favor Technique

Many girls who would be appalled at the idea of assuming the director's role can receive equally unfavorable results by using the opposite ploy: being insufficiently involved. One type of woman feels that by simply consenting to have an affair with a man she has done him such a tremendous favor she is not obliged to contribute anything else. As a result, other than lying prone in all her loveliness, she does about as much to inspire her fellow performer as a Greek statue. If there is an occasional sign of life from her, it is usually in the form of an admonition not to leave any bruises on this heavenly body, not to muss the beautiful locks, not to hold it too tightly, and so forth. Or she may attempt to experience vicarious thrills by hearing him describe his feelings while making love to her. "Do you like my breasts?" she may ask. Or, "Do you like to make love to me?" (As she lies so still only a necrophiliac could find her exciting.) If she brings up the question of being in love, it is only to ascertain if he loves her and how much. Reciprocity is out of the question.

Akin to the doing-him-a-big-favor performer, though less obnoxious, is the doing-my-duty girl. She tends to surrender not out of desire or need but out of a feeling of obligation, either because someone has taken her out a given number of times, or spent a particular sum of money, or perhaps even proposed marriage. Without warmth or enthusiasm (and at times with the stoic resignation of a lamb being led to slaughter) she submits. Period.

How to Be (Too) Good in Bed

While in my experience most women aspire to be good in bed, some girls' concept of good could more aptly be called goody-goody, and too much of a goody-goody thing could be bad. To play this role effectively, you should plan to play the bedroom scene with your halo undisturbed and virtue unblemished. Since this requires that she never sink to the "sinful" level of her co-star, it becomes almost impossible for them to find common ground in the sex scene, and the production flops under its own purity.

To portray the character in this morally superior part, begin with the notion that everything to do with sex, including the most basic procedures vital to the simplest performance, is vulgar—unclean. Then, after undressing underneath the covers, turn your head disapprovingly if your partner fails to do the same.

Your attitude primer here should be based on a belief that the human body in the nude is dirty, that he would lose respect for you if he saw yours and you would be defiled by the sight of his. Once in bed, he should also be cautioned against any attempt to become unnecessarily familiar—trying to caress you "disrespectfully" or fondle you "excessively." Give him the impression that practically all regions of your anatomy are off limits to the touch except the hands, arms, and, if handled with care, the waist.

Even after the actual act is in progress, maintain a certain air of decorum. Stop him mid-motion if he tries to take advantage of the situation and vary from the dry, tight-lipped kissing routine you have rigidly forced on him during your courtship. Keep remembering that the mouth is full of germs, that tooth-decay bacteria can be transferred, and hark back to the memory of those boys in the ninth grade who spoke disparagingly about girls who liked to French kiss. Regard as unseemly anything but total silence or the usual type of Orphan Annie or Mickey Mouse conversation during the sex scene. Consider any attempt on his part to verbalize the sensation he may be experiencing in poor taste; if ever he is so indiscreet as to use any four-letter words to communicate some idea or feeling, murmur, "Disgusting!" In general, proceed on the belief that the sex scene is actually too indecent a vehicle for you to be involved in; make your main objective neither to derive pleasure nor to give it, remembering constantly that the only thing which separates man from the rest of Creation is his ability to rise above his carnal interests.

Reversing Possible Sex-Scene Gains

Sometimes, despite your best neurotic efforts before, during, and after the sex act, and even the apparent collaboration of fate to help ruin it, it turns out a smashing four-star hit. (One reliable source testified that despite a leak in her protagonist's water bed and her most diligent endeavors, her sex scene earned rave reviews ["Passion was undampened," were her words]. And another swears that not even an ex-wife's persistent doorbell-ringing—she having spotted her former husband's car below and been anxious to discuss an alimony arrears crisis—could limit the passion of her rousingly successful sex-act finale.)

Experts attribute such phenomena to a mysterious chemical interreaction, certain complementary spiritual "X" factors, or just one of those things. In fact, no one knows the real answer, but when it occurs the danger to any aspiring loser in love is clear.

Therefore, when it becomes apparent that in spite of all

your efforts the "act" was a big success (a moderate success, or even a flop that he seems to be taking in stride), no time should be lost in trying to reverse the situation. Obviously, the better it was, the greater the emergency—the applicable Kennedy principle being: The extent to which sex was enjoyed relates proportionately to the urgency with which the affair must be destroyed.

Getting in the First Word

One proven method for nullifying possible sex-scene advances is by getting in the first word-blow. The sooner this can be accomplished, the better. Following are some dialogue guidelines to aid you at this pursuit.

The "Well-I-Guess-I-Won't-Hear-from-You-Any-More" (Self-Fulfilling Prophecy) Dialogue

This dialogue is particularly recommended if your sense of insecurity and lack of self-acceptance has you convinced that no one could want you for anything except to have his way with you in a passing sexual relationship. Or, as a friend of mine used to declare after the latest didn't-call-back statistic was resentfully (but happily) recorded: "All he wanted was my body." Also, this dialogue could prove helpful if you submitted so quickly that you suspect that he could not have the proper respect for you.

YOU: Well, I guess I won't be hearing from you any more after tonight.

HE (*caught completely off guard as he relaxes, about to light his post-sex cigarette*): Won't hear from me any more? What ever gave you that idea?

YOU (*seizing on the fact that he did not even bother to contradict your insightful remark*): Well, now that you've gotten what you want . . .

HE (*interrupting*): What do you mean, "Gotten what I want"? Aren't you being foolish to . . .

YOU (*interrupting his interruption, and noticing that he is beginning to drop the earlier pretenses and call you a fool for the first time*): Well, I'm not surprised that you think I'm a fool, since I've certainly behaved like one. But at least I'm getting wise to myself now.

HE (*hoping to change the subject and the tone of the conversation*): Darling, I move for a postponement of our first lovers' quarrel in favor of a romantic musical interlude. Any special album that you'd like to hear?

YOU (*with increasing pique on sensing that he has the nerve to expect a diplomatic, smooth ending to this one-night fling, which he clearly considers too inconsequential to rate even an argument*): Play anything you think appropriate. Look under "Swan Songs for One-Night Stands." Or how about, "First He Loved Her Then He Left Her."

The "Am-I-As-Good-in-Bed-As-She-Was?" Dialogue

Another good post-sex dialogue is to invite a comparative analysis of your sexual proficiency with that of his last girl friend. Background work for this approach should involve finding out as much as possible about his former love, preferably by interrogating someone who expounds on how perfect and gorgeous she was.

The scene begins immediately after dangerously good sex when he is lying on his back, hands folded under his head, dreamily looking up to the ceiling.

YOU (*naturally assuming he is thinking about "her"*): If I ask you something, would you tell me honestly?

HE (*playing the part of a knight of old*): Anything, my fair princess. You have but to command me.

YOU: Am I as good in bed as [let's call her] Gloria was?

HE (*already abandoning his faithful knight role*): Gloria! How in the world did she get into this?

YOU (*noticing how excited he gets at the mention of her*

name): I know she has a very sexy figure and her breasts are larger than mine . . . and I hear she doesn't wear a bra . . .

HE (*embarrassed, but still trying to be reasonable*): Darling, Gloria is the last thing in the world I want to talk about now. I haven't seen her in weeks, and I don't plan to.

YOU (*convinced that the gentleman doth protest too much [if he doesn't it is also a sure sign that he still loves her] and noticing that he has refused to give you a direct answer, obviously because she is better in bed than you are, not out of a sense of propriety*): I know you're still in love with her and I understand. I'm just curious to know how she was in bed . . . and why did you two break up anyway?

HE (*perhaps thinking that Gloria is beginning to look better every moment by comparison*): Look, there's really nothing more that I can contribute to this discussion.

YOU (*encouraged by signs of impending rejection, and for good measure*): Well, it's obvious to *me* that you only want *her*. So anyone else is just wasting time with you.

The Serious-Girl-Anxious-to-Settle-Down Dialogue

Another dialogue found to be very effective in nullifying any sex-scene gains is the following, which should be launched into almost before a man duly impressed by your performance in bed can catch his breath.

According to reliable reports one skillful failure with a reputation for being a sensational under*cover* girl has nevertheless deftly escaped any lasting relationships with the faithful use of this approach.

HE (*tenderly gathering you in his arms after an affair so fantastic it should be recorded in verse*): Sweetheart . . . I'm not one for superlatives but . . . tonight . . . I wish I had a page full.

YOU (*stroking him gently but meaningfully*): Oh, darling, I only hope I made you as happy as you've made me, because you must know that you're very important to me.

HE (*holding you closer*): Actually, I wasn't so sure, you always seemed so reserved and . . . serious, I never pictured you so uninhibited, so responsive. So wonderful.

YOU: But you're right, darling. I am serious . . . *terribly* serious. And what I want most of all is to settle down and try to make just one man happy.

HE (*suspecting an impending nomination for an office he has not seriously considered filling, relaxing his lover's hold somewhat*): But . . . you're still young . . . you've got plenty of time to make plans for something like that.

YOU (*insensitive to his subtle attempt to discourage you*): Yes, my love, but I'm anxious to have children while I'm young, so I can grow up with them.

HE (*to himself, "Don't 'my love' me, because if you have any kids by me they'll be out of wedlock." But for lack of anything else to say*): Well, I suppose you're right.

YOU (*encouraged*): Do you like kids?

HE (*thinking "Yes, someone else's" but saying*): Doesn't everyone but W. C. Fields? (*Suddenly remembering he has to get up early the next day, he excuses himself, turns his back, and goes to sleep.*)

Testing, Testing

The atmosphere of even the most romantically perfect after-sex ambiance can be toxified with this deadly pollutant approach. And since the concept can be used in numerous post-sex situations and locations, if immediate negative results are not forthcoming the prognosis for eventual failure is still encouragingly bright.

For greatest effectiveness with this method, it is necessary to bring to it belief that men want to use you just for sex and then leave—the same conviction that serves so well for the Getting-in-the-First-Blow Dialogues. In this case, however, indications are that the man in question likes you a lot—even after sex—and does not appear to be turned off by your usual neurotic behavior and tactics.

Since you have managed to be rejected by other men who have seemed to like you, though, you will resist being impressed by positive appearances, as you will not be satisfied until you can establish that someone *really* likes you. Inasmuch as you have been put down so often in the past and have such a low opinion of yourself, you have a special need to be *truly* liked. Therefore, you must administer a series of tests to seemingly sincere prospects. Since you come to the project convinced that you are defective and no good, common sense tells you that it is not possible for anyone to really like you, so that your true objective is to keep testing any likely candidate until—exasperated—he fails, thus confirming your suspicions and providing the rejection you sought.

The "I Have to Leave Now" Test

Here is one standard test to apply whenever you are experiencing a tender after-sex glow and begin to suspect that he might *really* like you. I will present this test in the form of multiple-choice, in order to test *your* progress in mastering the attitudes and techniques of rejection fulfillment advanced in this book. In the three dialogues below, you are to select which response (Tom's, Dick's, or Harry's) to your post-sex announcement, "I have to leave now," proves that he *really* likes you.

The mood is tender, and Tom (or Dick or Harry) is being more attentive than ever, when suddenly:
1.

YOU (*testing him to see what he will say*): I have to leave now.

TOM: All right, dear, I'll get dressed and take you home.

2.

YOU: I have to leave now.

DICK: Oh, darling . . . why do you have to go so soon?

YOU: I have something important to do first thing tomorrow.

DICK: I'm doing something important right now . . . stay a little while longer, won't you?

YOU: I really can't.

DICK: Okay, honey, I'll take you home right away.

3.

YOU: I have to leave now.

HARRY (*tenderly kissing you*): Perish the thought . . . how can I let you leave me?

YOU: But really, I must go. I have something . . .

HARRY (*interrupting*): I agree you have something. And that's why I want you to stay. (*Smiles.*) Besides, my door operates on a time clock and it can't be opened before tomorrow.

YOU: Seriously, I must go . . .

HARRY: Seriously, won't you please stay?

If you have become as proficient in the development of your skill at rejection fulfillment as I hope you have, you will know that none of the above men has passed the test to prove that he really likes you. *Tom* was obviously anxious to get rid of you. (Brush aside the possibility that he might only want to be accommodating.) *Dick* pretended not to want you to go just enough to be polite. *Harry* was selfish and inconsiderate, thinking only of himself and completely disregarding your wishes.

Devise your own tests for every possible occasion, always keeping in mind that the series does not end until you have successfully tested your target out of your life.

Psychological Warfare

Since men are usually very much influenced by our society's tendency to equate manhood and general worth with sexual prowess, they are understandably sensitive to anything that seems to reflect on this. Therefore, most men are prime targets for psychological preemptive attacks that subtly undermine their confidence in their ability to perform effectively.

The most important thing to remember here is not to be obvious, because the object is to make the man in question insecure and tormented by the *possibility* that he is sexually inadequate. (If he is not planning to call you any more—which you must always assume—this haunting possibility will give him something to mull over while you mull over why he never called you back.)

Here is one post-sex suggestion you could stage:

The scene begins as he has settled down and is lying back like the cat that just swallowed the canary, lighting a cigarette after having mumbled some perfunctory remark about how much he enjoyed his victory.

YOU (*smiling at him adoringly*): You know, darling, I think you may be smoking too much.

HE (*unsuspecting*): Too much? Actually I've cut down a lot. Only smoke a pack a day.

YOU: Oh, really? I just thought . . .

HE (*curious*): What makes you think I smoke too much?

YOU (*noncommittal*): Oh, I don't know. It just occurred to me that . . .

HE (*beginning to think he has caught a whiff of something*): You never remarked about my smoking too much before.

YOU (*in the calmly condescending voice men are supposed to use to humor and reassure emotional women*): Really, love, it's nothing to make a federal case of, it's only that I seem to remember having read somewhere that smoking *can* affect your sex life.

191

HE (*the impact of your statement having struck target like an enemy rocket in a troop compound, but still trying to scrounge around in the debris for something to salvage*): What's the matter? Didn't I . . . satisfy you . . . when we . . .?

YOU (*noting with pleasure that his cat-that-swallowed-the-canary look has now become the helpless, somewhat vacant expression of the walking wounded, damning him with faint praise*): Oh, yes, darling . . . you were wonderful . . . really, very nice . . . but it's probably just that you would have been more relaxed at your house than here.

Some of the other staging areas you might use from which to launch your guerrilla assaults could be:

1. A casual inquiry around the extent of his past sexual experiences, implying that you suspect they are limited.

2. Confession that sex is not everything and that your main attraction to him has always been spiritual anyway.

3. Introducing—after observing his sexual performance—the name of a girl friend that you would like him to meet.

4. Engaging in some light but teasing banter about his performance, especially if you feel he takes his sex dead-seriously. (Example: "Boy, that's some hip movement you feature in bed (*giggling*); you're good enough to be an Egyptian belly dancer (*tittering*) . . . favorite of the King . . . (*planting a patronizing kiss on his forehead*) . . . I'm going to call you Fatima from now on.")

The Post-Sex Postmortem

If you have a preference for destructive tactics that you can pretend are constructively motivated, you should love this approach. With it, disregarding the generally accepted theory that it customarily takes a period of adjustment before maximum mutual fulfillment is forthcoming, you em-

bark on a "constructively" critical analysis of everything
that took place during the just completed sex scene.

To set the right tone for this one, it is a good idea to "encourage" the prospect with the confidential aside that your
last boy friend seemed at first to be completely hopeless
when it came to sex. Add, "Even worse than you." Then
say, "With time and frank discussions of the difficulties, he
finally overcame his awkwardness and became an okay
lover."

Starting with that premise—that there is hope for everyone, even him—and citing some past lover's superior performance in the same situation as a guideline—you might
begin:

YOU (*softly, as he appears to be getting drowsy after
a relation he realizes was imperfect but feels was par for the
first time*): I'm sorry it wasn't so good, honey.

HE (*feeling that you are basically compatible and will
be able to work it out*): Oh, I'm sorry too, baby. But I
promise I'll make it up to you. (*Drowsily closes his eyes.*)

YOU: You know, the trouble was you started too soon.

HE (*dozing off*): Huh? What did you say, darling?

YOU: I said that you started too soon, before I could get
aroused. Tom and I had a formula—he would kiss me,
arouse and stimulate me, but he would never actually
begin until I asked him to.

HE (*waking up a bit on hearing the name and methods
of an old master*): Oh, really?

YOU: And you know, while we're making love, how you
caress my breast? Well, I find that distracting.

HE (*wondering if he did anything right*): Gee, I didn't
realize. I'll remember not to do it next time. (*Turns over to
go to sleep.*)

YOU (*unable to let well enough alone, and somewhat
resentful that he doesn't seem to be accepting your helpful hints with proper enthusiasm*): And when you cli-

maxed, that howl you let out sounded like you were getting ready to throw a karate chop.

HE (*thinking that would probably be a good idea, but pretending to be asleep*): ZZZZZZZZZZZZ.

Loving Him to Death, or Killing Him with Kindness

At the opposite end of the spectrum lies the sure-fire method I call loving him to death. The idea here is to find your beloved so great in bed that you are unwilling ever to let him out.

To accomplish this, after sex for the second time that night (or third, or the number required), when it is obvious that he is about to throw in the towel and is unable to respond to the next bell, you lead the cheers for a return bout. Since most men feel that protecting their good-lover image is essential in protecting their ego and general worth, the good money is on you to receive a favorable response to your demand that he go another round. Finally, however, there will come a time when he is so pooped he couldn't take to battle if not only his ego but his life depended on it. And yet he will still feel inadequate and completely emasculated if you continue to call on him and he finds he is unable to respond.

Bear in mind that the above are only guidelines which, as with all we illustrate and suggest, can and should be adapted to your own talents and neuroses. Remember, too, that if any do not work at first as hoped, try, try again. They can be used singly or in any combination. If applied properly, and with true neurotic devotion, without question even the most rousingly "successful" horizontal encounter can be reversed, and the goal of nonfulfillment once again achieved.

Conclusion (1)

Voilà!

I do hope that by now you have deeper insights not only into your present self but into your past behavior. And, it is hoped, into your future. For if till now you have only used your neurotic talents part time, or haphazardly, henceforth and forever more you have the bases for applying them full time, on all occasions.

While I have no desire to try and resume here the main theses and thrusts of this magnum opus, I would like to leave you with a list of what I call "Classic Offenders and Old Standbys," to which you can refer quickly and easily on urgent occasions. You might think of it as your Special Emergency Kit.

1. If ever your target makes an unflattering reference to his family (wife, children, parents, *et al.*), hasten to concur. Better: try to improve on his derogatory remarks.

2. If ever your target's best friend asks you out on the sly, accept, but be sure to tell the "friend" not to rat on you to You-Know-Whom.

3. If ever your BF finds himself in a financial bind, offer ready sympathy, then lend him some money (if it's a relative pittance), making sure thereafter to tell one and all of your generosity.

4. Saddle your BF with a pet name you know he loathes and insist on using it in public. Or when you call him at the office.

5. When he calls you, continue reading or watching TV as you talk, spicing your end of the conversation with appropriate non sequiturs, shrill laughter, oohs and ahs, and other phone language meant to make him know he is not the focus of your undivided attention.

6. *Always* supply the punch line of any story or joke he is telling others.

7. If you must argue (and you must), make sure to argue in front of others.

8. If ever he turns serious, interrupt his conversation with repeated peals of laughter and phrases such as "You sure are a card!" or words to that effect.

9. If he has weak points (and who's perfect?), harp on them day in, day out.

10. Play chameleon, changing your mood as often as you change your clothes.

11. Change your clothes at least five times a day, preferably when your target is waiting for you.

12. Always compare him in one way or another with a predecessor, and find him wanting. (That way, you'll soon find him missing.)

13. For Hot-and-Heavies, play Victorian.

14. For Decent-Upstandings, play Linda Lovelace.

15. Never look into his eyes when he is talking to you: in private places, look around, as though for something, or someone, more interesting. In public places, table-hop.

16. Be quick to anger, slow to forgive.

17. Never be ready on time.

18. In the presence of family (his) or friends (yours or his) order him around like a servant (giving him a foretaste of the bliss he may expect if he persists with the likes of you).

19. Never underestimate the power of hair curlers, remembering the equation: HCpu-2HCpr.*

20. Never tell the truth when a lie will do just as well.

While the above does not pretend to provide the alienation power you can hope to acquire through careful study of this volume, it can nonetheless stand you in good stead

---

* Or: Hair curlers worn in public equals twice the value of hair curlers worn in private.

when, for whatever reasons, your neurotic potential seems suddenly to have deserted you. I have always urged students in my courses in Advanced Neurosis to commit them to memory. Those who did so have, without exception, told me time and again how grateful they were to know these gems by heart.

Conclusion (2)

If, after careful application of as many of the principles and tactics outlined in this work as apply to you and your neuroses, your target continues to show patience, sympathy, and understanding, to love and cherish you despite— or perhaps because of—your faults, relax and enjoy him.

In which case, take this volume and pass it on to some more needy friend.

If that advice strikes you as incompatible with the express purpose of this work, or represents a failure on the part of the publisher, editor, and author to discharge their responsibilities to the public, know that such is not the case. For the subject of this book is the alienation of men, and in those rare instances where its teachings fail, know that you are no longer dealing with a man: you clearly have found a saint.